Leading *in a* Diverse & Conflicted World

Previous Books by Dr. John P. Fernandez

*Race, Gender and Rhetoric: The True State of Race
and Gender Relations in Corporate America*
(Published by McGraw-Hill)

*The Diversity Advantage: How American Business Can Out-Perform
Japanese and European Companies in the Global Marketplace*
(Published by Lexington books, an imprint of Macmillan, Inc.)

Managing a Diverse Workforce: Regaining the Competitive Edge
(Published by Lexington books, an imprint of The Free Press)

Human Resource Forecasting and Strategy Development
(Published by Quorum Books)

The Politics and Reality of Family Care in Corporate America
(Published by Lexington Books, D.C. Heath and Company)

*Survival in the Corporate Fishbowl:
Making It into Upper and Middle Management*
(Published by Lexington books, an imprint of Macmillan, Inc.)

Child Care and Corporate Productivity: Resolving Family/Work Conflicts
(Published by Lexington Books, D.C. Heath and Company)

Racism and Sexism in Corporate Life: Changing Values in American Business
(Published by Lexington Books, D.C. Heath and Company)

Black Managers in White Corporations
(Published by John Wiley & Sons)

LEADING *in a* DIVERSE & CONFLICTED WORLD

Crucial Lessons for the 21st Century

DR. JOHN P. FERNANDEZ

Edited by Malia Bruker

Global Tree Publishing
701 West Allens Lane
Philadelphia, Pennsylvania 19119

Cover design and interior formatting by Mayfly Design (mayflydesign.com).
Visit the author's website at www.drjohnpfernandez.com.

FIRST EDITION
Leading in a Diverse & Conflicted World is available as an eBook through Amazon.com.

ISBN-13: 978-0615921372
ISBN-10: 061592137X

This book is dedicated to my four daughters, Paige Julia, Sevgi Mary, Eleni Julia, and Michele Gertrude, who have greatly impacted who I am as a person and leader. Their multiracial, multiethnic, and multilingual backgrounds have given me tremendous insights into how difficult it can be to attain acceptance and equality in the United States and around the world.

My four sisters, Gertrude, Ann, Joyce, and Sandra, helped me appreciate the challenges women face in so many aspects of their lives, which, as a man, I can only continue to try to understand and appreciate.

This book is also dedicated to my long-term supporters, mentors, and friends who have had significant impact on my personal and professional life. Without them I would not have been able to write this book or the nine previous. I am deeply grateful and indebted to Lydia Allen-Barry, Dr. Harry Aponti, Belva Greenwich, Magali Iglesias, Tony Jenkins, Melanie Littlejohn, Tony Marino, Dick McCormick, John McCormick, Jillian McWhirter, Louis K. O'Leary, Larry Paul, Alex Silva, Chuck Snowden, and Connie Sousa.

Table of Contents

Introduction *1*

Chapter 1: Being a World-Class Leader
is Much More Difficult Than You Think 21

Chapter 2: Proactive Inclusion® Based
on Globaltree℠—A Strategy for The 21st Century 39

Chapter 3: Human Evolution—
How Rational and Objective Have We Become? 49

Chapter 4: Stereotyping is Human But Extremely
Dangerous—How Explicit and Implicit Biases
and Stereotypes Impact Human Interactions 67

Chapter 5: The Complexity and Subjectivity of Human Cultures ... 99

Chapter 6: Bureaucracies And Hierarchies—Two Necessary Evils . 127

Chapter 7: Cultural Clashes Among Diverse Teams 163

Chapter 8: The First Step Toward Change—Know Yourself! ... 195

Chapter 9: Creating Healthy Communication
Among Diverse Employees 223

Chapter 10: Key Reminders for Becoming
a Great 21st Century Leader 245

Acknowledgments *257*
About The Author *259*
Index *261*

Introduction

"If we really want to know who we are and how we can solve the problems humanity faces, we must try to understand not just human natures as they are today, but also their origins."

– Paul Ehrlich

As a civilization, humans have walked on the moon, cured diseases, created a Declaration of Human Rights, and developed computing systems that have opened up endless possibilities for the generations to come. Humanity would not have progressed economically, socially, or politically if we had remained in our small and isolated family clans possessing the same norms, values, and, ultimately, the same worldview. Just as human society benefited from diverse cultures, experiences, and skills coming together, corporations that work to include and value diversity in this increasingly interconnected world will achieve and sustain a competitive advantage.

In order to do this, leaders must start by truly understanding the numerous and complex conflicts that have existed within all levels of societies and organizations for thousands of years. Many leaders are unable to meet the high standards that followers expect; not because they lack aptitude, but because leadership education, development, and training do not cover key areas needed to deal with these conflicts.

Regardless of country, data shows that 60–70 percent of employees report that the most stressful aspect of their jobs is their immediate leader. A 2005 article in the *Harvard Business Review* found that 55 percent of leaders in the workplace were associated with below-average performance. Over the twenty-five years of this study, only 15 percent of leaders showed a consistent ability to manage innovation and organizational change. It is clear that our world is rapidly shifting. Leaders who are able to embrace change will direct motivated, confident, and diverse teams, and will bring significant, sustained successes to their organizations.

This book will provide a holistic, non-traditional approach to understanding why so many employees lack confidence in their leaders. It will offer strategies and tools to improve knowledge and skills for those in leadership positions so they may be more effective and successful in this rapidly changing, diverse, and conflicted global climate.

Over the years, numerous books have been written about leadership and the ways to become an effective leader, but crucial areas have not been given enough attention. These areas include personal self-reflection, human evolution, key characteristics of the human brain, implicit and explicit biases and stereotypes, the complexities and subjectivities of our cultures, and the true nature of bureaucracies. Due to the omission of these issues, many authors and scholars assert unfounded and inaccurate assessments about the true nature and abilities of human beings. These inaccurate evaluations negatively impact a leader's ability to develop and effectively manage diverse world-class teams, as they often fail to integrate the essential foundations of successful organizations: trust, respect, empathy, and ethics. Similarly, most companies do not truly comprehend the difficult demands and complex challenges leaders face today. This ignorance leads to the misplacement of a great deal of leadership training, education, and development.

Furthermore, to be most effective it is important to recognize the disconnect between our leaders' requirements in today's corporations and employees' expectations of them. Our ancestral roots have created a preference for leaders with egalitarian hunter-gatherer values like fairness, honesty, benevolence, generosity, humility, kinship, compassion, collaboration, ethics, and self-sacrifice. Unfortunately, many of today's organizations are led by managers whose values and behaviors markedly diverge from these qualities. This divergence stems from traits of self-centeredness, dishonesty, and greediness, which are the main causes for frustration, alienation, and conflict between leaders and followers, and the reason for many leaders' consistently low marks.

This book also presents the realities and challenges that leaders throughout the world will increasingly face and must overcome to build world-class organizations. It examines the roots of our social behaviors based on both the biological and cultural evolution of human beings. An understanding of these evolutionary processes can teach leaders the ways in which people come together and interact in both positive and negative ways.

In the chapters that follow, original research and data on leadership, team effectiveness, communication, diversity, stereotypes, and cultural issues collected by Advanced Research Management Consultants Global (ARMC Global) are presented to enhance the education and development of leaders as they face the new and unique challenges of the twenty-first century. The information and skills described will assist leaders to more effectively understand, manage, and lead diverse and complex organizations.

This book has evolved from my experiences over the past forty-five years working, studying, educating, and consulting with global and local corporations, universities, governments, non-profit organizations, and independent practices. I have distilled themes from numerous ARMC Global surveys, focus groups, and interviews. The concepts and solutions have been tested and revised over the course of working with, training, and developing many leaders and employees from different countries and cultures. Associating closely with these individuals has helped form many of the ideas within this book.

These ideas have also been shaped from my personal life experiences of growing up in an extremely poor, uneducated, multiracial immigrant family, surrounded by White, working class and middle-class families. Promoting the ideas of fairness, real opportunities in all aspects of society, and complete acceptance of those who are different has been a personal and professional quest.

Finally, having lived and worked in several different countries on four continents has helped me foster a greater understanding of the diversity of the world in which we live. These experiences have shown me that while cultures and regions around the world vary in many ways, there are basic human values that all people share.

Chapter Summaries

Chapter 1: Being a World-Class Leader Is Much More Difficult Than You Think

Throughout the centuries there have been conflicts between our ancestral expectations of a leader's role and the modern leadership style commonly practiced. As the world has become more interconnected, and as organizations have brought together different cultures, these conflicts have increased. Chapter One explores how these conflicts often become more complex in the workplace and how they create challenges for global leaders. Schools, universities, MBA programs, and executive or leadership development programs devoted to leadership enhancement do not adequately prepare leaders to be successful because they do not address key concepts related to our human biology and history. The focus has been on administrative, technical, and professional skills, and not on human relations and personal skills. Leaders are not provided with strategies to understand how their own life experiences affect their values and the lens through which they view the world. Nor are they provided with real opportunities to understand their own strengths and weaknesses as human beings. Leaders often lack education about the keys to human behavior: our true nature, our thought processes, and our evolution.

Humans are not as rational or objective as we are taught to believe and it is crucial that leaders accept this. The reality is that without a lot of work and constant self-awareness, many humans are in fact subjective and irrational much of the time. To guide people effectively leaders must understand the reasons behind this irrationality, such as implicit and explicit biases, stereotypes, and the cognitive tricks our brains play on us.

With its numerous information processing systems working simultaneously, the human brain is more complex than the fastest super computer. Like computers, our brains can experience errors and glitches as we attempt to understand and manage the multiple layers and many sources of information constantly barraging us. Leaders must recognize these common misfires in order to deal effectively and efficiently with the conflicts that exist between human beings and their organizations, corporations, societies, and families.

Effective leaders must also understand the complex and subjective nature of culture in order to develop a context for interpreting individuals' behaviors. To reach this understanding, a leader must know not only about the evolution of the bureaucratic structure, but also how it has impacted human behavior. Only with an appreciation of the evolution of human nature can leaders and their employees start to build healthy relationships and better diagnose organizational and team issues. In turn this will produce more suitable and relevant solutions for leading and growing their diverse organizations.

Leaders must build certain knowledge bases, but we also must recognize the increasing demands that are placed on leaders by the people following them. Leaders are expected to excel at all the traditional management skills such as finance, strategic planning, and negotiation. They are supposed to be excellent writers and communicators who demonstrate integrity and high moral character at all times. We routinely expect our leaders to free not only themselves but also their people from all forms of stereotyping and biases. We ask them to be proactively inclusive and create an environment built on trust, respect, empathy, and ethics. Leaders are expected to do the right thing, even when it is not always clear what that is or how to do it. According to Thomas Teal, the former senior editor of the *Harvard Business Review*, employees often insist that leaders "should be our friends, mentors and guardians, perpetually alert to our best interest." We ask all of this from our leaders without realizing that most of them are personally and culturally unable to do so. Finally, most leaders lack the organizational time, support, and resources, both professional and financial, required to understand and deal with these types of issues effectively and efficiently.

In summary, one key reason for the lack of world-class leaders is that their education, training, and development focuses too much on technical and professional proficiencies and too little upon human natures and awareness of personal values and behaviors. The emphasis must shift in order to assist leaders in understanding their own human strengths and weaknesses, as well as the natural shortcomings and strengths of the brain and our human natures.

Chapter 2: Proactive Inclusion® Based on GlobalTREE℠—a Strategy for the 21st Century

Chapter Two defines the ways that Proactive Inclusion® and GlobalTREE℠ (Trust, Respect, Empathy, and Ethics), two concepts developed by the Advanced Research Management Consultants Global team, are crucial in minimizing human conflicts in societies and corporations while making them inclusive, efficient, and effective environments. As corporate leaders constantly position their organizations to become or remain leading competitors in the local and global market-places, it is increasingly clear that one key to their success is their ability to develop diverse, critically self-aware, and cul-turally competent employees who can function effectively on both global and local high-performance teams to pro-duce quality products or services at competitive prices.

Although many corporations believe they value open, honest communication and inclusion of people of differing backgrounds, perspectives, and work styles, there are obvi-ous disconnects between the stated values and actual behav-iors and practices. At the same time it has become apparent that in order to create global, world-class, innovative teams in which far fewer of these disconnects occur, it is neces-sary to create proactively inclusive environments based on Trust, Respect, Empathy, and Ethics (GlobalTREE^{SM}).

GlobalTREE^{SM} is a strategy that works to create an atmosphere in which employees are encouraged to learn from their mistakes and take corrective actions. It holds individuals accountable for successes and shortcomings, not only in results but also in behaviors. A key feature of this strategy requires leaders to become intimately familiar with their own strengths and weaknesses as human beings. They must relinquish the myth that we are all rational and objective all the time.

Proactive Inclusion$^{®}$ is a strategy based on Global-TREE^{SM} in which the broad spectrum of peoples' widely varying skills, perspectives, backgrounds, experiences, abilities, and styles are proactively recognized, appreciated, valued, respected, and fully utilized, regardless of country of origin, region, race/ethnicity, religion, language, age, sexual orientation, gender, style, or any other differentiating factor. This strategy will enable corporations to build global, world-class teams that are stronger because of their ability to truly capitalize on diversity of thoughts and ideas. Proactive Inclusion® effectively maximizes marketplace opportunities, products, and services throughout the world, and improves employee relationships by allowing corporations to anticipate and more effectively respond to change.

This chapter will present a seven-step process for implementation of a Proactive Inclusion® strategy based on GlobalTREE℠. The purpose is to assist corporations in looking beyond the superficial and guiding them to seek out, hire, retain, and fully utilize the best talent, skills, thoughts, and ideas to serve increasingly diverse and demanding customers.

Chapter 3: Human Evolution—How Rational and Objective Have We Become?

Chapter Three discusses our biological and cultural evolution and their impact on the human brain. It is fruitless to argue about which of these evolutionary processes has a greater impact; it is more important to understand how they interact and influence one another.

Our cultural evolution has developed much faster than our biological evolution. The human brain today is similar to our brain tens of thousands of years ago, but the daily routines and practices of our cultures scarcely resemble those of ancient times. The uneven evolutionary speeds between technical and cultural evolution have significant negative impacts on humans. For example, we have the ability to make various chemicals that harm the environment, but we lack the social will to control the destruction of our environment by the improper use of these chemicals. Alternatively, we were able to develop the automobile, which has contributed greatly to the growth of world economies, but the slower pace of our cultural growth has inhibited our ability to respond to the automobile's contribution to global warming and environmental degradation. Regardless of the plentiful data about global warming and its danger to our earth and our civilization, we lack the will to devise long-term effective solutions to minimize it.

It has taken millions of years for the brain to evolve to its current state. Our brains have gradually gotten bigger and developed specialized structures not seen in other species. We have learned how to walk, talk, eat, and show emotion without ever really thinking about how we do any of this. Each of these seemingly simple operations requires our brains to make billions of complicated connections and computations in nanoseconds. Unless all of these billions of connections occur seamlessly, and the chemical compounds that ensure brain function are totally balanced, our brains can easily misfire.

As a result of our slower biological evolution, our brains tend to operate as though we were living forty thousand years ago in a hostile and dangerous world. Thus we still have the tendency to make swift, uninformed decisions, many of which we base on subconscious stereotypes. Much of our behaviors are based not on conscious thought, but rather on unconscious ideas of which we are not even aware. Because of this, our perceptions do not always reflect reality.

This logic shows the fallacy of the oft-repeated mantra of the corporate world that "perception is reality."

Chapter Three considers how our uneven evolutions impact subconscious thoughts and behaviors to prevent us from seeing the world, other humans around us, and ourselves objectively. The challenge for leaders is to help the people they lead to understand and appreciate these realities. Such understanding is a critical precursor to elimination of negative predispositions and creation of environments that minimize human conflict. This chapter shows the limits of the brain and how those limitations negatively impact our relations and decisions. Unless we become aware of these shortcomings and learn to overcome them, the ability for leaders to build proactively inclusive societies and organizations is greatly limited.

Chapter 4: Stereotyping Is Human but Extremely Dangerous—How Explicit and Implicit Biases and Stereotypes Impact Human Interactions

This chapter examines the concepts of classism, caste, socioeconomic elitism, racism, sexism, ethnocentrism, religious intolerance, homophobia, xenophobia, and other biases and prejudices. These social ills have evolved from the tribal tendencies of early humans to favor one's own particular group and at the same time covet other groups' land, people, and resources. We justify such favoritism and our desire for other groups' resources through use of stereotypes and biases; we claim that we are better than they are, and therefore more deserving.

One of the outcomes of the long evolution from our hunting and gathering days to our modern world is that humans still have an extremely strong preference to favor our kin or "pseudo" kin (e.g., our colleagues in our business unit versus colleagues in other business units). People use stereotypes and biases to justify this in-group favoritism and, on a grander scale, to eliminate or minimize competition from another cultural group in economic, political, social, and personal environments. We human beings have developed some very practical reasons to justify creating stereotypes and biases toward people who are different from us, regardless of how we define those differences.

Biases and stereotypes can be both implicit and explicit. Explicit biases and stereotypes are those that we have thought through and have made a conscious decision to include in our belief and value systems. We endorse and support them. Implicit biases and stereotypes are unconscious. We state strongly that we do not endorse or support them. As a species, we are usually unaware of how our unconscious minds control our thoughts and behaviors. In fact, our brains are programmed to collect and store data that we consciously call upon at times, but more often call upon unconsciously. As such, our implicit biases and stereotypes affect our behavior without our knowledge.

This chapter will present stereotypes collected from thousands of employees from a number of countries with responses of their very first thoughts on "types" of people, such as politicians, Jews, overweight people, Brazilians, Muslims, women, and Nigerians, as well as people who seek mental health services. Numerous studies conducted around the world about implicit and explicit biases and stereotypes in varied categories such as race, gender, height, skin color, names, religion, school attended, community raised in, weight, and more will be cited to give the reader a keen sense of the depth of stereotyping and the negative impact it can have on members of corporations and societies. ARMCG also conducted many surveys using Harvard's Implicit Association Test (IAT), which measures unconscious biases in a number of areas. The results, acquired from several thousand leaders and employees from around the world and presented in Chapter Four, confirm other study results. This chapter will also provide methods for readers to examine their own implicit and explicit biases and stereotypes, as well as strategies and best practices for minimizing biases and stereotypes through personal action.

Chapter 5: The Complexity and Subjectivity of Human Cultures

Culture can be defined with three simple but extremely important considerations: the values, beliefs, and assumptions on which our behaviors are based. A society determines its culture by developing workable solutions to the problems associated with its environment. Among the numerous factors that impact an individual's cultural identity are three major influences: ethnicity, language, and religion. They are woven into our sense of self and influence how we see the world, and therefore impact our ability to understand one another and ourselves. The degree to which we acknowledge and embrace our similarities and differences defines how effectively we can build creative, productive, and proactively inclusive teams, organizations, and societies.

While we as adults are "free thinking" and capable of making personal decisions, the range of conceivable values, beliefs, and assumptions we hold are defined by the societies in which we were raised and, to a lesser extent, in which we live as adults. As a result of our socialization, we learn how to be people of color or White, Basque or Catalonian, Japanese or Korean, Hausa or Yoruba, English or Scottish, Hindi or Muslim, Brazilian or Venezuelan, French-Canadian or English Canadian, men or women, Conservative or Progressive. We acquire a sense of the worth of our social group and of ourselves during our earliest contact with other members of our family, our peers, and our teachers, as well as from what we read, conversations we overhear, and our daily observations.

It is crucial to remember that simply because a person is born and raised in a particular cultural group does not mean that the person will believe or buy into the cultural values of that particular group or organization. Thus in order to build relationships in the workplace, leaders cannot make assumptions about people based on their apparent cultural group. To assume that one major dimension of culture captures a person's identity is to greatly oversimplify, and therefore miss important information about the person. Instead, leaders must get to know the individual on a personal basis. In addition, since many of us are multicultural and call on a variety of cultures to survive and prosper in this world, leaders must understand the complex and varied nature of cultural identity.

This chapter presents examples of cultural nuances from a number of diverse countries. The reader's variety of reactions to these nuances will depend on his or her own life experiences. When ARMC Global tested reactions to the same nuances at seminars and workshops, we received responses ranging from reasonable and valuable to irrational and barbaric. Various missteps made around the world relating to particular cultural nuances illustrate the ease of offending people from different cultural groups. The ease in committing these offenses adds to the challenges in leading diverse organizations.

The information in Chapter Five will assist readers in breaking the stereotypical thought patterns that human beings naturally use. The insights provided can help readers better understand and build relationships with people from different cultural backgrounds.

Chapter 6: Bureaucracies and Hierarchies— Two Necessary Evils

Chapter Six explores the origins, necessities, and faults of the modern bureaucratic structure. Societies initially created the bureaucratic structure to minimize societal conflicts and create efficiency. At ARMC Global we propose a new organizational structure that is more appropriate and better suited for our current world and the true nature of the human being.

Bureaucracies evolved thousands of years ago due to the domestication of plants and animals and the convergence of human beings. Since the inception of agriculture, life has become more sedentary. As the production of food improved, surpluses began to be available for storage and distribution. The bureaucratic structure emerged in part to deal with surpluses fairly and efficiently, as well as to facilitate the coming together of people with no familial relationships. These new relationships required an efficient social structure to maintain harmony among people not otherwise bonded.

Sociologist Max Weber's ideas reflect the views commonly held by today's leaders. According to Weber, bureaucracies are indispensable in meeting the production needs of modern societies. They are characterized by specific rules and a hierarchical division of labor in which authority is inherent in the role, not the person. This codification and structure as outlined by Weber can work, but certain factors about human nature will consistently create conflicts within societies and their bureaucracies. A key source of conflict in a bureaucracy is its attempt to remove the humanity from human beings. Most bureaucracies are structured to treat people more as a means to an end than as an individual. In addition to all this, most bureaucracies possess only limited resources that must be used for all of the various and unlimited desires of all members in the organization.

Leaders can overcome these shortcomings by creating an organizational structure that effectively aligns with our human natures and offers better opportunities to create inclusive environments based on Trust, Respect, Empathy, and Ethics (GlobalTREE^{SM}). You will find such a structure outlined in Chapter Six. This model promises to build more efficient, productive, and responsive organizations and societies.

Chapter 7: Cultural Clashes among Diverse Teams

Chapter Seven looks at reasons why conflict and challenge manifest themselves in today's corporations. Most corporate and team failures are rooted in unproductive and unhealthy cultures rather than a lack of technical, professional, or business knowledge and skills. Data collected over the past thirty-five years illustrates where conflicts originate in teams and how they impact effectiveness. These data aid in understanding the challenges leaders will face when creating high performing, proactively inclusive, and diverse teams.

The impact of culture on corporations is most evident in mergers and acquisitions, especially those between corporations from different countries. These failures get a lot of media attention, such as the Chrysler/Mercedes or Lucent/Actel failures. However, a closer look shows that corporate failures based on cultural clashes are just as evident in companies that have not merged or been involved in acquisitions or partnerships. The cultural clashes occur among different business units, different organizational levels, and different leaders and employees. To avoid these types of conflict, this book offers six steps toward building more effective diverse teams, including personal self-assessment and the establishment of team values.

Often companies believe that conflict should not exist. While that would be ideal, conflict is inevitable. Chapter Seven makes the case for bringing conflict out into the open: you will find guidance on how to deal with conflict constructively, ten steps for resolving conflict, and a case study of effective conflict resolution based on ARMCG's consulting experience. The various tools cited in this chapter will provide you with insights to assess your own potential challenges in working on diverse domestic and global teams.

Chapter 8: The First Step Toward Change—Know Yourself!

Chapter Eight looks at how each corporate culture is a combination of individual cultures. Thus, while the organization has a major responsibility to facilitate what we at ARMCG define as Proactive Inclusion®, nothing will change until all team members recognize their responsibility to create change within themselves and the organization. Humans excel at pointing out others' shortcomings, but find it exceedingly difficult to acknowledge their own. Yet the first step toward building GlobalTREE℠ is for each of us to take stock and understand all of our strengths, as well as our weaknesses. Due to our complex nature as humans, in order to truly understand ourselves we must use a variety of tools and methods. The assessment tools presented in this chapter also provide feedback on different aspects of character. One tool that assists readers in understanding their own experiences and the way they see the world is the Life Environment and Values Inventory (LEVI). ARMC Global developed the LEVI while consulting at Bank of America in order to help clients open up to having a dialogue on race, class, gender, religion, and other sensitive subjects. The LEVI focuses on the impact of such factors as geography, family structure, wealth, education, gender, and religion to show how they each affect the values, beliefs, and behaviors that determine how we perceive and interact with the world.

In Chapter Eight you will also find fourteen detailed skills to help you succeed in multicultural environments, including learning how to be comfortable with ambiguity and learning how to be more flexible. Included are the steps needed to achieve these skills and to become more productive members of corporations and societies.

Chapter 9: Creating Healthy Communication among Diverse Employees

One significant problem in facilitation of GlobalTREE[SM] is that even humans from the same culture and family are not the best communicators in both the personal and professional worlds. We all understand the importance of effective communication, yet we rarely give much thought to this complexity. Combined with the shortcomings of the brain and our implicit biases and stereotypes, communicating effectively becomes increasingly difficult. This chapter provides knowledge to assist leaders, regardless of country of origin, in more effective communication. Improvement can only come by first examining our own values, beliefs, stereotypes, strengths, and weaknesses. The idea behind these suggestions is to help make communication empathetic, respectful, and ethical in a clear, specific, and concise manner, while also minimizing misinterpretations and bridging gaps that can lead to conflict. The effectiveness of this message lies in its ability to clearly reach all readers, regardless of their cultural background.

While there are many barriers to effective communications, this chapter discusses the most important ones, such as language differences, clashes in communication styles among different cultures, snap judgments, and poor listening skills. You will find tools to successfully establish effective communication and listening skills that can be used in most cultural settings and with most people. Each point is based on the establishment of mutual GlobalTREE^SM (Trust, Respect, Empathy and Ethics) between individuals.

Chapter 10: Key Reminders for Becoming a Great 21st Century Leader

Chapter Ten summarizes and enhances the key recommendations that have been presented throughout the book about how to create proactively inclusive, diverse, and world-class working environments and teams.

This chapter considers the major trends in leadership development seen in organizations around the world. It explores the shortfalls of leadership assessment systems like competency frameworks, and explains some fundamental issues in the ways most people, organizations, and educational institutions think of leadership. Experience tells us that leaders must not only focus on the business issues related to technology, finance, innovation, and administration, but they must also focus more pointedly on the softer skills that depend upon a knowledge of how to deal with humans.

The economic crises of the past few years demonstrate the excesses in which corporations, societies, and people can entangle themselves because of greed and unethical conducts. The huge disparities and differences between the "haves" and "have nots" will continue to create challenges for leaders, as will the growing interconnectedness of this diverse world and the speed with which news and information are disseminated. As discussed in this final chapter, there are three key ways to effectively deal with the continuous changes in business today: understand humans, understand yourself, and commit to the principles of trust, respect, empathy, and ethics.

CHAPTER 1

Being a World-Class Leader is Much More Difficult Than You Think

A truly world-class leader must constantly display the combined skills of Elizabeth I, Barack Hussein Obama, Catherine the Great, Sigmund Freud, Mother Teresa, the Great Houdini, Mahatma Gandhi, Sitting Bull, Susan B. Anthony, Tecumseh, Warren Buffett, and Nelson Mandela. It is no surprise that most managers seem to underperform.

If you were to ask a thousand people to define leadership, you would get a thousand different definitions. Each answer would be based on personal life experiences, values, and individual worldviews. One reason leadership is so difficult to define is its dependency on the varying challenges our societies and organizations face. As we have evolved, we have created notions of leadership that are based on such factors as population size, climate, natural resources, and population diversity. The traits of outstanding leaders are much easier to define. These people have developed the skills to build a substantial foundation in trust, respect, empathy, and ethics. These values constitute the Global-TREE^{SM} system. By emphasizing trust, respect, empathy, and ethics they are able to effectively coordinate all the resources of a diverse workplace to achieve societal, organizational, and individual goals.

Many of today's leaders insist that they support the values that comprise GlobalTREE^{SM} and lead companies that are meritocracies: their organizations are already diverse, value and encourage proactively inclusive ideas, and maintain highly ethical structures. These individuals perpetuate the myth of human objectivity and rationality and believe it is strongest in themselves. According to these leaders, all of their decisions are made in the best interests of employees, customers, and society in general, and are never based on their own personal desires. Although these leaders purport to operate with the highest moral and ethical standards, it has become clear that there is a huge disconnect between their claims and the reality of their behaviors. This chapter will explore the reasons for this disconnect and the difficulties in being a world-class leader.

The History of Leadership

To understand the difficulty of being a leader, it is first important to realize how today's version of leadership emerged. We must remember that early human history, characterized by thousands of years of very tight-knit, egalitarian living, has shaped the ways we respond to leadership today. Historically, we strove for leaders with traits that could ensure survival for small hunter-gatherer tribes. These leaders were chosen based on competence, generosity, fairness, and compassion. Although much of the world has changed since then, our innate feelings about what makes a good leader have not, and the leaders of today do not match up.

Around thirteen thousand years ago small tribes began evolving into larger bands of people who were not related to each other. The development of agriculture and the domestication of animals led to two major results that dramatically changed the size and structure of communities: a settled lifestyle and surplus food. While human survival was once tied to a nomadic way of life, agriculture required that humans establish permanent residences. In turn, adherence to an agricultural way of life led to an increasing surplus of food, which brought together groups who would not have previously associated. All that held these populations together were kinship and an investment in each other's fate. The norms of reciprocity and fairness required that individuals depend on others and return the favor in kind. These communities were small, around 150 people or less, and group decision was the ultimate authority in maintaining peace and prosperity. Living conditions were fundamentally egalitarian and leadership was consensual, democratic, and transitory. There were no formalized leadership roles; the best hunters and warriors exercised more influence on their society's decisions, but the community limited even that power. Safety was found in numbers and no one could survive alone in that resource-limited world.

As these villages grew, they became too complex for

everyone to fully participate in the decisions impacting the community. Therefore, organized leadership became a fundamental necessity. These growing populations required societal rules and laws to solve not only distribution of surplus food, but also the competition over limited resources. Communities that best coordinated their efforts to resolve internal conflicts were the ones that survived and prospered. Communities that failed to do so ultimately disappeared through war, famine, or other catastrophes. A new bureaucratic model emerged to account for growing populations, but it conflicted with our innate leadership psychology, and continues to do so. We evaluated leaders then, as we do now, using our early egalitarian standards such as fairness, honesty, generosity, ethics, kinship, competence, humility, compassion, and self-sacrifice. People across various societies do not view attributes like greed, deceit, dominance, or force as beneficial or desirable leadership qualities, but unfortunately these characteristics have been continuously supported and even rewarded in our bureaucratic structures and are commonly seen in many of today's leaders, especially those at the top.

The State of Leadership Today

One reason for the increased presence of ineffective leaders is the fact that the consequences of poor leadership are not nearly as severe as they once were. Today's leaders know they would never be sent into the wild where isolation would certainly lead to death, as was the punishment for poor leadership in early human societies. In many cases, all that can be done today is to vote these individuals out of office, fire them, or force retirement with a hefty compensation package, none of which are easily accomplished. In the very rare but most severe cases, leaders can be sentenced to short prison terms, but none of these available punishments hold the same consequences as fighting for one's life.

Of course we do not wish today's inadequate leaders to be subjected to the cruel, extreme punishments of our ancestors, but without significant consequences for bad behavior or poor decision-making, leaders often do not function at the level they should, or even at the level they expect of their employees. In many companies, the values that are posted on the walls are very rarely those that actually walk the halls. One convincing piece of evidence to support this claim is based on data Advanced Research Management Consultants Global has collected over the past fifteen years from employee studies in companies around the world. When asked to rate the degree to which "the senior leadership team lives the company values" on a scale of 1–10 with 1 being very poor and 10 being excellent, the average score employees gave their leaders was 5.9 out of 10—a very mediocre score.

In forty-five years of studying corporate behavior and more than thirty years conducting leadership and management surveys as a consultant, I have found that inadequate leadership is not just a current trend. As Division Manager of Human Resources at AT&T Corporate Headquarters from1984–1986, I conducted studies that showed roughly 50 percent of its leaders were considered failures when they were promoted to the next managerial level. In more recent surveys conducted in the U.S.—in 2005 and 2012 by

ARMCG—over half of the employees' responses showed negative perceptions of their middle and senior managers.

Obviously there are additional factors contributing to this extreme disconnect between leaders and their employees. Roughly 75 percent of Europeans and Americans say their opinions of business leaders have worsened due to the current economic crisis. The numerous scandals that have hit companies around the world have caused the general public to believe that the majority of senior leaders are grossly overpaid. Many of the recent corporate scandals originated in part because leaders began to see themselves as the public does; they too believed they had "absolute power." Yet despite this belief in their own power, leaders do not take responsibility for their personal and organizational failures. Very often the government or lower-level managers become scapegoats for these failures.

In today's corporate climate, many leaders seem to act like the gods in Greek mythology, primarily seeking aggrandizement, glory, and reward; they put their personal needs above their employees and customers. These individuals blindly pursue short-term financial rewards instead of focusing on long-term sustainability and customer satisfaction. One example of such a person is Kenneth Lay of Enron, whose business decisions impoverished thousands of employees, stole livelihoods, gutted retirement accounts, and tore people apart with stress and anguish. There is little doubt that several Enron employees took their lives because of the greedy actions of its lavishly compensated leaders. Similarly, Bernie Madoff was seen as a strong and effective leader, and his interpersonal skills enabled him to gain the trust of many, some of whom bought into his schemes. Unfortunately for his clients, Trust, Respect, Empathy and Ethics (GlobalTREE^{SM}) were replaced by his ability to finesse numbers and look good on CNBC. The events that transpired with British Petroleum and the Gulf of Mexico oil spill give us yet another example of leaders putting short-term financial gains over concern for the environment and overall human population. And of course many of the root causes of the current global financial crises can be traced back to the greed and short-term focus of the financial industry's leaders, as evidenced by the enormous losses of companies like Chase, Citibank, and Barclays.

Scandals of this sort happen all over the world. Volkswagen, Siemens, and Daimler, three of Germany's largest corporations, have been wracked with integrity issues. Additionally, Klaud Zumwinkel, the former CEO of Deutsche Post in Germany, was arrested on charges of tax evasion. A Royal Bank of Scotland branch was violently attacked by individuals who were incensed by the shortsighted, financially dangerous decisions made by the former head of the company. In Brazil, China, India, and Japan, many corporate and political leaders were forced to resign because of their greedy and corrupt behaviors. In France unhappiness with corporate leadership reached such a critical point that employees have taken to kidnapping their bosses. These disgruntled employees have held hostage senior managers at Sony, Caterpillar, and 3M. Finally, in what sounds more like a Hollywood movie than reality, a UBS AG private banker smuggled diamonds into the United States, an act that severely damaged the global reputation of corporate Switzerland. These examples demonstrate only a portion of the corruption and incompetence of our many leaders, but the list is seemingly endless.

The gap in pay between workers and executives is widest in the United States. A recent report by the Institute for Policy Studies helps put this issue into a real-world context. Currently, CEOs in the U.S. make an average of approximately 325 times as much as rank-and-file employees. If minimum wages had risen in the same manner as salaries of top management over the past twenty years, it would be $22.61 per hour. Instead, the federal minimum wage remains $7.25 per hour. Although many leaders today are perceived as greedy, detached, or incompetent, their own self-worth tends to be immensely high. A good example of the extreme greed and narcissism are the huge bonuses executives give themselves, regardless of their companies' financial states. It seems that many corporate leaders have become intoxicated by their power over the scores of people working below them. The lavish offices, huge expense accounts, and corporate jets all feed this image. The homogeneous, elite environment in which many of these leaders work, socialize, and live compounds this situation. To overcome the trappings of this kind of power takes a person of great discipline, self-awareness, and integrity.

Despite the examples above, we know that not all leaders are bad. There are some individuals who exhibit more of the ancestral, community-minded leadership traits that allowed our earliest societies to function. James Sinegal, the founder and former CEO of Costco Wholesale Corporation, kept his salary at $350,000 per year from 1999 to 2012, when he stepped down as CEO. He also insisted on giving his employees high wages and good healthcare packages. Similarly, a business owner in Florida laid herself off in order to save her company and her employees' jobs. Individuals like Warren Buffett and Bill Gates show characteristics of ancestral leaders by giving much of their fortunes to benefit humanity. Examples like these bring about hope and show that there is promise for our future.

The Effects of Poor Leadership on Employees

In a routine work climate survey ARMCG conducted, 60–70 percent of employees in the organizations we surveyed reported that dealing with their immediate leader was the most stressful aspect of their jobs. Following the employees' own values and beliefs, the most frequently cited factors that influenced their business decisions were directly related to leaders. Participants responded on a scale of 1–10 with 1 being "to no extent" and 10 being "to a great extent," and their responses were averaged.

To what extent do you feel the following factors influence your business decisions?

Your Personal Norms, Values, and Beliefs	8.2
Company Demands	7.6
Leaders' Demands	7.5
Senior Management Behavior	7.4
Your Performance Goals	7.1
Pressure to Produce Strong Numbers	6.5
Work Stress	3.6
Family Stress	3.5

As the data clearly demonstrates, a leader's influence can be extremely powerful. The considerable influence that leaders have on the decision-making processes of their employees points to a simple but significant concept: the leader's value system is one of the most important factors shaping the environment and culture of a company. Whether that value system is a healthy one based on GlobalTREE^{SM} or a debilitating one characterized by dishonesty, narcissism, and greed will determine the long-term health of any organization.

Throughout history we have seen that a good leader is not just followed, but respected, and sometimes even adored. This is because these kinds of individuals fulfill a basic human desire to be led by someone who will ensure survival and prosperity. The consistently high failure rate and low marks received by leaders confirm this mismatch between the leadership we crave and the leadership we receive. However, this is not the only problem. There have been and always will be conflicts between humans and their organizations, as well as between leaders and their followers. This is due in part to the fact that most followers believe they can do better jobs than their leaders and also that they generally believe they deserve more compensation and benefits than they receive. In today's corporate atmosphere, it is only natural for humans to question the motives of their leaders while constantly looking out for their own interests. But we have the knowledge and ability to change this.

Addressing Inherent Organizational Conflicts

An organization's basic function is to mobilize human, natural, technical, and financial resources to produce goods or services for various customer bases. However, these objectives do not take into account many of the human dynamics that are required to make an organization function. Regardless of the job title a person holds, humans generally resist being treated as a means to an end. As we interact, we do so as whole beings, bringing to each situation our own unique characteristics from our exclusive set of genes and our personal culture. With those traits, we also bring our own agendas and problems. Employees want to be treated as individuals, not just simple tools used to carry out corporate goals. Therefore it seems only logical that conflicts will arise between a corporation's goals and an employee's aspirations and needs. It is imperative to recognize this disparity and follow steps to solve these issues to prevent them from undermining the entire process.

Many of today's companies are hierarchies, embedded with numerous institutional matrices and subject to pressures from the environment. We can think of these companies as adaptive social structures that face arising problems simply because the company exists. When viewed in this manner, these organizations are simply social instruments used to help meet their members' aspirations and needs. Because individuals can have such a strong influence on their organizations, it is crucial for leaders to understand the nature of bureaucratic structures as well as the nature of humans, the latter being perhaps the most important because of our endless complexities and uniqueness.

The Chartered Institute for Professional Development (CIPD) in England published a classic report agreeing that many companies suffer from a shortage of effective leadership. Particularly disturbing was CIPD's conclusion that despite companies' investment in leadership training, this training does not deal with the particular necessary skills leaders must have to be effective. Additionally, the report concluded that there is a severe lack of beneficial training and development in the personal spheres of leaders, which is an extremely important facet of what determines leadership character and style. This dearth of personal exploration results in a lack of self-awareness, crucial information about one's evolution, and people skills. Attaining this knowledge is not easy and takes a tremendous amount of personal strength, hard work, and extreme patience, but is a critical first step in becoming an effective leader.

Realizing this, Harvard professor Thomas Teal has developed an accurate definition of management that takes into account the reasons why middle management receives much of the blame for an organization's faults. Teal claims, "At the most basic level, a manager is someone who creates an environment that enables a group of people to get their jobs done. So, at that most basic level, people are the most critical component of effective management. And yet, when one calls to mind the typical qualifications and training programs for managers, people skills don't come in high on the list." Therefore, it seems obvious that a big part of the leadership problem has to do with the *way* our managers are educated and developed. In recent years, an MBA has become the most important and desired management credential, but the vast majority of these programs only focus on "core" business skills like economics, marketing, and strategic planning. In order to initiate change, business schools and other development programs must shift their attentions to the disparity that exists between what we want from our leaders and what we get.

A New Model for Developing Our Leaders

Take a minute to consider the leadership and development programs you have either heard of or experienced. How many focused on assisting leaders in developing a clear understanding of their values, beliefs, and behaviors through reflection on their own life experiences? Were leaders helped to better understand their explicit and implicit biases and stereotypes? How many programs focused on understanding the various human natures? Were managers educated on the complexities and subjectivities of culture? Finally, did any programs teach leaders how to overcome and effectively manage the realities and issues brought about by these complexities? My guess is that very few curricula were designed to accomplish any of these important principles.

By failing to provide proper training or development, we are asking the impossible from our managers. As Teal asserts, "The troublesome fact is that mediocre management is the norm.... The overwhelmingly most common explanation is capable management is so extraordinarily difficult that few people look good no matter how hard they try. Most of those lackluster managers we all complain about are doing their best to manage well."

Richard Bolden, a research fellow with the Centre of Leadership Studies at University of Exeter, supports Teal and points out another problem. Bolden addresses the uselessness of leadership competency frameworks. These frameworks are lists of defined skills and abilities that each company requires from its leaders. They rarely consider the various definitions for each skill or the fact that each individual has a personal understanding of the definition. And most important, these competencies are static and attempt to solidify behaviors that are actually quite fluid. They do not take into account the complex interactions of human beings and the unique situational aspects of each and every human encounter in and outside organizations.

Disregarding these very important truths about human behavior, companies measure their leaders against those competencies to see where additional training is required. While most of these leadership competency guidelines focus on the leader's professional and managerial skills, there is a lack of attention to the fact that most normal human beings tend to look outward and try to make sense of the world and their place in it. Bolden's study shows that most leaders' greatest concerns in regards to themselves involve trust, personal beliefs, ethics, and moral courage, four key points that are missing from most competency frameworks. Bolden's research supports our belief that companies sideline the emotional, ethical, and cultural aspects of leadership when in fact they should focus on these aspects.

Shifting away from generic business skills toward personal development seems to be a key solution to our problem. Yet these generic skills are not all we ask of our leaders; we also expect them to be excellent writers, speakers, persuaders, and communicators. And the list does not end there. Over the past thirty years demand has increased for leaders who demonstrate qualities that define leadership, such as integrity and character. Adding to that list are the responsibilities of being a proactively inclusive leader, creating a GlobalTREE^{SM} environment, and eliminating discrimination of any kind. We routinely expect our managers to free both themselves and their people from every type of bias and stereotype. As Teal argues, "We insist that they should be our friends, mentors or guardians, perpetually alert to our best interests." We once had leaders like that, thousands of years ago, and we still want them today.

We ask all of this from our leaders, despite the simple fact that some are personally or culturally incapable of meeting these expectations. We seem to forget that most leaders lack the organizational support and the appropriate knowledge and skill development they require in order to understand and deal with these types of issues effectively and efficiently. We constantly expect our managers to do the right thing, even when it is not always clear what that is or how to do it. Further compounding this problem is the lack of accountability regarding the implementation of those critical skills. It is no wonder that being a world-class leader of tremendous diversity, both internally and externally, is more difficult than anyone could have imagined.

Considering all of this information, ARMC Global compiled a set of fifteen crucial leadership proficiencies, each of which will be discussed in this book. This list addresses the gaps that Bolden and others have recognized in other competency frameworks. The adoption of these proficiencies will help inform and develop truly world-class leaders.

1. Awareness of personal experiences and their contribution to one's worldview.
2. Basic understanding of human evolution and human natures.

3. Knowledge of the ways leadership has evolved.

4. Appreciation of the ancestral characteristics of leadership that most humans desire.

5. Recognition of the connection between genetic and cultural evolutions.

6. Comprehension of the capacities and limitations of the human brain.

7. Knowledge of the ways the subconscious mind can control the conscious mind.

8. Understanding that humans often make snap decisions based on limited information.

9. Recognition of the cognitive tricks human brains can play.

10. Understanding that perception is not always reality.

11. Appreciation of the complexity and subjectivity of one's own culture, as well as others'.

12. Understanding of the reasoning behind implicit and explicit stereotypes and biases.

13. Acceptance that meritocracies do not really exist.

14. Comprehension of the reasons and ways bureaucracies evolved.

15. Full acceptance of the values of proactively inclusive organizations where the environment is based on GlobalTREE[SM] (Trust, Respect, Empathy, and Ethics).

Conclusion

It has become quite clear that for leaders to be successful they must be completely self-aware, committed, emotionally intelligent, and fully knowledgeable of human natures and bureaucracies.

What the world needs today is proactively inclusive leaders. These leaders affect the ways their employees see themselves by helping them evolve from self-interested individuals to members of a larger, almost familial, group. These individuals model trust, respect, empathy, and ethics; they emphasize the group's similarities in terms of goals, objectives, and common interests; and they constantly celebrate their personal characteristics as unique human beings. Under the direction of an ideal leader, everyone in the organization knows that his or her best interests coincide with the best interests of the group, and that both are taken into consideration. This is not shown through words, but rather the leader's behaviors and ability to share successes and failures fairly. The need for this type of leadership is greater today than ever before in human history because of the growing interconnectedness of our world and the social and cultural complexities associated with such a historic convergence. Needless to say, there is much work to be done.

CHAPTER 2

Proactive Inclusion®
Based on GlobalTREE^{SM}—
A Strategy for the 21st Century

"If we are to achieve a richer culture, rich in contrasting values, we must recognize the whole gamut of human potentialities, and so weave a less arbitrary social fabric, one in which each diverse human gift will find a fitting place."

– Margaret Mead

The first step toward becoming a world-class leader is creating the right workplace environment. In addition to the ideas presented in the Introduction and Chapter One about humans, leadership, and bureaucracies, for leaders to be effective in this diverse and conflicted world, they must also understand, appreciate, and implement a strategy we call Proactive Inclusion® which is based on GlobalTREE^{SM}.

In this chapter I will define these two strategic concepts in greater detail.

One of the major issues in business today is the tendency toward workplace value-systems that are based on extreme individualism, selfishness, and exclusion rather than team-work, inclusion, and innovation. Companies proclaim to have open and honest communications, transparent agendas, and appreciation of creative and inventive thinking. In reality, honest displays of these ideals are too frequently perceived as "rocking the boat."

To address these types of dysfunction, corporations must change their cultures. Although most organizations and individuals acknowledge the need for change, the amorphous and vague nature of cultural change is challenging. Very few individuals know where to start, and most of us expect someone else to take responsibility for affecting change. Significant cultural change requires active participation by everyone in the organization and is successful only with the total support of leaders.

GlobalTREE℠: The Tree of Life for World-Class Corporations and Organizations

GlobalTREE℠ is a system that was developed at ARMC Global to help address and minimize the many dysfunctions in the workplace. This concept parallels the ideals of the "green movement" we see throughout the world. The green political ideology aims to create an ecologically sustainable society for future generations by raising awareness of personal choices and how they affect the environment. GlobalTREE℠ works in similar ways to create positive, forward-thinking workplace environments that enable corporations to thrive and succeed. While the foundation of GlobalTREE[SM] is based on the values of Trust, Respect, Empathy, and Ethics, it is fitting that the sum of these parts adds up to a word of metaphorical importance: the tree.

Every tree is individual, each one with unique size, leaves, bark, fruit, shape, and color. The earth needs this kind of diversity to sustain life around the world in different climates and conditions. People are just as unique; like trees, we have all been shaped by our specific environmental challenges and opportunities. The fundamental concept of GlobalTREE[SM] is that just as the earth benefits from diverse trees, corporations will also benefit from diverse people, thoughts, and ideas. By creating an environment based on Trust, Respect, Empathy, and Ethics, an organization looks beyond the superficial and truly seeks out, hires, retains, and utilizes the best talent, skills, thoughts, and ideas to serve increasingly diverse and demanding constituencies.

Trees help make earth livable for millions of species. By producing oxygen and reducing toxic carbon dioxide, trees play a crucial role in human survival. Trees also create a moderating influence on otherwise harsh landscapes. They cool the earth, block heavy winds, create shade, and stop soil erosion. Similarly, GlobalTREE[SM] works to improve workplace environments by making them more supportive, proactively inclusive, innovative, and rewarding. The ideals of GlobalTREE[SM] help reduce the toxicity that arises from racism, sexism, ageism, classism, homophobia, greed, group favoritism, and other such societal ills. Global-TREE[SM] creates the proper conditions to develop a healthy and productive environment; it is only when this environment is created that cooperation and creativity are appropriately nurtured and sustained.

In addition to the environmental benefits that trees offer humans, many of them also provide us with life-sustaining fruits. GlobalTREE^{SM} is capable of the same types of productivity in the corporate world. One barrier to efficient production stems from the ongoing conflicts between employees' desires for rewards and the limited resources available for those purposes. GlobalTREE^{SM} will help employees realize the value and importance of their work and contributions, not just the value of recognition. When these internal conflicts are minimized or removed, corporations can better capitalize on the various skills and ideas coming from their diverse group of employees. Ultimately, GlobalTREE^{SM} provides a much longer lifecycle for productivity by ensuring lasting creativity, innovation, and competitiveness. This allows the corporation to better meet the needs of all constituencies while becoming more successful every day.

The trunks of trees are the foundations for stability. They are the conduit between the water and nutrients in the ground and the leaves, flowers, and fruit on the branches. Similarly, a strong and innovative leader committed to GlobalTREE^{SM} is an essential stabilizing factor in any company. Leaders create and transmit the corporation's values and missions, ensuring that they are practiced throughout the organization and are instilled in the ultimate service or product. Leaders are the centerpiece that connects all parts of a corporation and holds members of the organization accountable. Without strong leadership based on GlobalTREE^{SM}, corporations cannot flourish long term.

Obviously, there are places on our planet that have no trees. These regions typically are oppressively hot or unbearably cold and little life is able to grow there. The people who live in these areas are forced to adapt their lifestyles to survive the harsh conditions. Living beyond a bare sustenance level in these lands is nearly impossible, and rarely viable. There are certain corporations that live in this kind of environment. When GlobalTREE^{SM} is not present, either heated and open conflict or cold and hidden animosity exists among the employees, making these environments unbearable and unsustainable. GlobalTREE^{SM} can help create and foster an environment that ensures the inclusion and respect of all types of people, allowing a company to truly capitalize on the diversity of perspectives to develop innovative ideas and enhance competitiveness.

Throughout the past forty-five years of work, it has become clear that no organization can truly prosper if it does not constantly work to build GlobalTREE^{SM}. This effort requires extreme and deliberate dedication. As human beings, we all have distinctive experiences and values that help us see the world in different, unique ways. If we do not apply the ideas of GlobalTREE^{SM} to improve our understanding of how we relate to the world, corporations and their employees will remain stunted, never reaching full potential.

Proactive Inclusion®: A Global Corporate Strategy Based on GlobalTREE^{SM}

Many people carry negative connotations for "strategies" like "diversity," "inclusion," and "affirmative action" in the U.S., and "positive discrimination" in other countries like

Brazil, India, Canada, Malaysia, and the European Union. These terminologies and programs raise red flags for many who are not in a position to benefit from them. The term diversity means vastly different things to different people and provokes a variety of reactions. Some assume that it refers solely to race and gender; others believe it is a form of reverse discrimination; and still others think it is favoritism for those protected. Those with more positive perceptions of diversity usually understand it to mean variety or heterogeneity. Many organizations began to move from the term diversity to the term inclusion, with less intense but similar reactions. However, neither of these terms, nor the strategies associated with them, adequately describe the depth, breadth, and power of a world-class, proactively inclusive societal and business strategy based on GlobalTREE℠.

ARMC Global has tried to manage these differing perceptions and has developed Proactive Inclusion®, a new globally relevant model to assist leaders. This ideal carries no negative connotations and accurately describes an active global strategy. Since Proactive Inclusion® is based on GlobalTREE℠, it fosters an atmosphere in which the values and thoughts of someone who does not traditionally fit in are truly esteemed and utilized. Our model encourages employees to take risks, learn from mistakes, and take corrective actions. Proactive Inclusion® holds every individual accountable for all successes, shortcomings, and personal behaviors.

At ARMCG we have created a guideline of seven steps that must be taken in order to implement Proactive Inclusion®. A commitment to these steps will allow an organization to reach its full potential for success.

Step 1: Define and implement a plan that will help your corporation comply with all laws and regulations of the country of operation, as well as the values of the company in which you are working. When there is conflict, make decisions based on your respect of all humans as equal and valuable employees and customers.

Step 2: Assist employees in understanding and appreciating the interconnectedness of local and world populations and businesses.

Step 3: Using multiple methods, honestly and transparently assess the current corporate cultures and how they enable, change, or impede the Proactive Inclusion® of diverse people, styles, experiences, thoughts, strategies, etc. Thoroughly assess how policies and practices such as recruitment, retention, performance appraisals, promotions, rewards, recognition, benefits, and training impact the ability to build GlobalTREE^{SM}.

Step 4: Develop a comprehensive business case for implementing effective Proactive Inclusion®. Ensure that all business unit leaders develop their own Proactive Inclusion® business case and regularly evaluate progress.

Step 5: In recognition that a business case alone is not sufficient, corporations must develop self-aware, culturally sensitive, and well-trained employees in order to experience all the benefits of Proactive Inclusion®. To do so, organizations must educate employees to understand the impact that life experiences have on values, views of the world, explicit and implicit biases, stereotypes, and the limitations of human beings. This knowledge boosts one's ability to produce timely, cost-effective, and competitive world-class products and services for diverse customers, while contributing positively to societal growth.

Step 6: Completely reshape the corporate culture by creating an organization-wide culture based on Trust, Respect, Empathy, and Ethics (GlobalTREE^{SM}). This will require a total overhaul of the education and development of leaders and employees at all levels. These initiatives should emphasize what human nature and behaviors are, not what we want them to be. It should also emphasize self-awareness and self-discovery. This assists in the integration of the broad range of diverse styles, viewpoints, thoughts, and approaches that make up a corporation. Ultimately, an entire redefinition of skill sets will be developed in order to truly understand how diverse markets can be proactively approached, developed, and served.

Step 7: Establish a post-bureaucratic organization based on Trust, Respect, Empathy, and Ethics (Global-TREE^{SM}). This will foster an environment in which every employee is valued and proactively integrated into all aspects of the organization. Constant self-reflection is necessary in order to do this, but completely worth the effort. Work is greatly enhanced and improved by reexamining organizational structures and tasks, and by redefining strategies, business practices, and products.

The primary focus of these steps is not only to rearrange the structures, but also to proactively change the cultures, thoughts, and behaviors. By putting our seven steps into action, organizations can do more than just assimilate; they can proactively change. Both local and global groups can unite to form something new, instead of merely folding one group into another and enforcing the old processes of conformity and agreement. In the past, societies demanded more assimilation and conformity to gain control, but today's markets have evolved to become heterogeneous and extremely global. Therefore, the only way to manage and capitalize on change is for the strategies to evolve as well.

Implementing Proactive Inclusion® based on Global-TREE[SM] requires strong leadership, exceptional role models, and extensive planning, not only on business matters, but also on human matters. It is important that leadership understand their own strengths and weaknesses, particularly their implicit biases and stereotypes, as they relate to the diverse domestic and global corporations they lead. These individuals must be totally honest about how their values have developed and the ways they can be reshaped. Once leadership fully adopts these concepts and holds employees accountable, innovation will spread throughout the company and allow for the GlobalTREE[SM] to truly bloom.

CHAPTER 3

Human Evolution—How Rational and Objective Have We Become?

"To understand our human natures in any depth requires knowing something of our prehistory and the mechanisms of both biological and cultural evolution."
– Paul R. Ehrlich

Chapter Three presents some very important concepts about the evolution of both human genetics and human culture. Although we understand a portion of what makes humans behave in certain ways, there is so much we do not yet comprehend. Very few people truly understand the basics of the human brain and how it impacts the ways we see the world and interact with people. In order to build more productive organizations and societies based on Trust, Respect, Empathy, and Ethics (GlobalTREE^SM), we need to take advantage of the knowledge available and really take the time to understand human complexities.

Human Evolution

Studies of early human history show that for tens of thousands of years, humans survived by hunting and gathering in small familial groups and then in small tribes. Those societies were comprised of families who understood one another's values, beliefs, and behaviors. They survived from day-to-day and were constantly moving to find habitable environments and sufficient food. Severe weather, the lack of sustenance, and dangerous animals made life extremely perilous. In order to exist in these hostile environments, people depended on each other; working as a group was paramount to survival. As a result, humans evolved into complex social animals who rely heavily on one another.

In the relatively short duration of human evolution, scientific and technological advances have contributed to the development of mega-cities. This expansion grew out of a need to accommodate exploding populations and to build increasingly intricate relationships and organizations. Over the past two hundred years we have become extremely innovative in the areas of technology, agriculture, health, and organizational structure. Regardless of these advances, we have made little progress toward understanding and solving human conflict within our societies. While many of these conflicts, both significant and trivial, are framed in moralistic, value-laden rhetoric, the vast majority of these disputes stem from the competition for economic opportunities, resources, land, minerals, food, water, and yes, people. All are limited in supply compared to human needs, both real and perceived.

Human conflicts impact not only those directly involved in them, but also the people who are regionally affected or dependent on the resolution of the issues in question. World War I and II, along with the Arab Spring of 2011, are classic examples of regional issues and conflicts that have impacted most of, if not the entire world. The financial crisis of the twenty-first century shows how intertwined the world is financially and economically. We are now in an age when it is abundantly clear that every person in the world is connected to every other person in the world; if we do not realize this and overcome the ethnocentricities we have developed, societies will meet insurmountable hurdles in our quest for further advancement. In fact, if we continue on the path of individualistic advancement and greed, societal destruction and economic catastrophe are very likely.

Biological Evolution

Life on earth in the form of simple cells began more than 3.5 million years ago. Human life in the form of the homo habilis of the *homo* genus began about 2.3 million years ago. All scientific evidence shows that human beings arose from a few families in Africa and essentially share the same genetic pool. As humans migrated from Africa to other regions, necessary changes evolved in the genetic material to make it easier for humans to adapt and survive in these new environments. Our genes are essentially still 99 percent the same, but humans developed different physical appearances—skin color, eye shape, or hair texture—to allow us to survive in varied climates.

As we have evolved, certain ethnic groups have also passed down diseases and disorders that are not as common in other ethnic groups; for example, cystic fibrosis is most common in Caucasians and sickle cell anemia is most common in people of African or Mediterranean descent. But many other genetic traits are passed down across all ethnic and racial lines. People of all races and ethnicities are born blind; others have Downs Syndrome, while others are lactose intolerant or allergic to bees. Likewise, skilled mathematicians, amazing artists, great athletes, and wonderful cooks exist in every society and ethnic group. These skills and characteristics are due in large part to their inherited genes, but are not necessarily related to their race or ethnicity.

It is easy to look around and see how vastly different humans are. Yet, the reality is that we all share the same basic biological wants and needs. It is essential to remember this while concurrently trying to understand how concepts like cultural evolution impact our growth as humans.

Cultural Evolution

Our cultures are the foundations from which our values develop. They produce the different responses we have to the varying problems facing our societies. Our culture is comprised of the values, beliefs, and behaviors we have learned from our families, institutions, and the environments in which we were raised. As individuals, our behaviors, thoughts, and ideals are due, in large part, to our early development in a particular culture. As we proceed through life, the environments in which we live and the people with whom we interact continuously influence us.

Both cultural and biological evolution have played important roles in our development as humans, and while we have extremely limited control over how we develop biologically, we have more control over how we evolve culturally. Cultural evolution can occur much quicker than genetic evolution. While genes are only passed biologically from one generation to the next, the ideas, behaviors, and values that make up culture are transmitted to all people moving in both generational directions, and also within generations. Germany is a good example of the possibility for rapid cultural change. During the past one hundred years, the country started two world wars, but over the past sixty-five years it has become a peaceful nation. Despite committing mass genocide at one point, Germany has now evolved to curb the kind of derogatory fervor that led to the Holocaust, including, for example, the development of exceptionally strong laws against hate language. For further proof of the possibility of rapid cultural evolution, consider the United States and its racial history. Only fifty years ago there was legal segregation in public buildings, marriage, education, employment, and housing. Now the same country has elected, and re-elected, the first Black President; to be more correct, the first racially mixed president. These examples show how vastly a culture can change over a relatively short period of time.

Of course there are also examples of human cultures that do not change; the seemingly endless conflicts between Christianity and Islam have been occurring for more than one thousand years. A similar lack of advancement is the inequality women still face in even the most "progressive" countries, never mind the dire status of women in countries like Afghanistan, Pakistan, Saudi Arabia, and some African and Asian nations. Broadly speaking, while cultural evolution seems stinted in these situations, it is clear that these are circumstances largely influenced by leaders and people in power, not the majority of people in the society.

It has become abundantly clear how impactful leaders are in fostering forward movement. But it is also apparent that any form of cultural change is very much up to the people within that culture. It is extremely important that every person is conscious of the resources we bring to support our culture's values, beliefs, and behaviors. As such, any society that adopts GlobalTREE^SM will be built on the meaningful and diverse contributions of all members of the society as they work to achieve the best human values such as respect, compassion, and generosity.

Genetics versus Culture

We have approximately 100 to 200 billion nerve cells, or neurons, in our brains, and on average there are approximately 100 trillion connections, or synapses, between them. That makes at least tens of thousands of synapses per cell. Because of these incredible numbers, it is easy to imagine that our brains could have difficulty making sense of these connections from moment to moment. Many people believe our brains have mostly preset connections that dictate behaviors and the ways we see the world. Although it is true that the brain has certain "programs" that have developed over millions of years by natural selection to ensure survival, humans are also capable of performing innumerable spontaneous actions and behaviors that are not programmed. So what factors determine our actions and behaviors?

Throughout our history, many scientists have believed our genes dictate our behaviors and that we are essentially hardwired to become the people we are. Some studies prove this by showing how an environment shared by children has no measurable influence on how those children grow into adults; siblings raised apart often share as many traits and characteristics as children raised together. Likewise, many of the variations among people in characteristics like intelligence and personality are not predictable from any obvious feature of one's environment.

Conversely, there are also many scientists who argue that our environment is the main determinant of our behavior. They point to examples of children who are separated at birth and brought up in different cultures. They note that even though these children come from the same parents and genetic pool, they will also pick up the behaviors, language, and cultures of the society and family in which they are raised. According to these studies, it seems that the range of behaviors seen in humans is not based exclusively on our genes, but on our cultural evolution as well.

These two constantly evolving notions of genes and cultures make understanding human natures one of the most difficult challenges facing leaders. Both sides of this debate have presented thorough and exhaustive research. After years of study, we conclude that human beings are a combination of the ongoing interactions of our genes and our culture. It is impossible to argue which has the greater impact on our behaviors because for now we lack conclusive scientific data. Furthermore, even in the simplest organisms, on a biochemical level, gene processes are not completely systematic and are affected by the random nature of chemical reactions. This genetic roulette becomes even more significant in an organism as complex as the human, leading us to understand that the two traditional notions of human nature and nurture must be augmented by a third contributor: chance. It is this unpredictability that makes us unique.

All this sets the stage for what we can expect from personal genomics. Even if we know the totality of genetic predictors, there will be many things about ourselves that no genome scan and no demographic checklist will ever reveal. Whatever genetic quirks incline a youth toward one niche or another will be magnified over time as she develops the traits that lead to the ability to flourish in an environment. Also magnified are the accidents of life (catching or dropping a ball, acing or flunking a test), which, according to the psychologist Judith Rich Harris, may help explain the seemingly random component of personality variation. The environment, then, is not a stamping machine that pounds us into a shape, but a cafeteria of options from which our genes and our histories lead us to choose.

Evolution of the Human Brain

Despite the important role of environment in our development as individuals, it remains equally important for leaders to gain a better comprehension of the brain and its functions, limitations, and abilities. Once we truly understand both the limits and possibilities of the human brain and stop buying into the myths we have created about the objectivity and rationality of human nature, we will be better able to solve the problems that exist globally and locally in our corporations and societies. Without this knowledge, leaders cannot fully appreciate the challenges in forming proactively inclusive and productive organizations based on trust, respect, empathy, and ethics (GlobalTREE^{SM}). A deep and complete understanding of the processing and operation of the brain is not necessary, but some basic concepts and knowledge about its functioning abilities and limitations is absolutely essential to help leaders understand how to better lead their organizations.

Neuroscientist John Allman observes that the human brain evolved in order for us to survive in a world full of hazards and threats to our survival. As he correctly notes, there would be no need for a nervous system if humans were immobile and our surroundings were predictable. Given the unstable nature of human life, our brains act as buffers against the variability of the environment in which we exist. Although that observation is constructive, there is still a wealth of information needed to be able to apply these scientific findings to our current issues.

As mentioned before, the evolution of our brains has been slow, and as a result, they greatly resemble those of our ancestors. It has taken roughly 2.3 million years for the brain to develop its current capacities, yet it is still neither entirely rational nor objective. Stripped down to our most basic capabilities, humans are only another animal species with biologically driven instincts that can be influenced by our cultural surroundings. Our brains still stereotype, make snap decisions in milliseconds, and tend to strongly favor our kin. The primitive "fight or flight" mindset that was required for survival in the more dangerous and brutish world of our ancestors is still wired into our brains and human natures. Unfortunately, that "fight or flight" mind-set we needed then is influencing our ability to make rational, objective, and unbiased decisions now.

We no longer need to make constant snap decisions to ensure our safety, yet we constantly deal with even the smallest issues in just that way. Think about the number of times you first see or meet a person. How frequently have you, on conscious or subconscious levels, made decisions in milliseconds about whether you like or dislike the person? These dynamics of snap judgments play out within corporations thousands of times a day. We have been socialized to make judgments about those who are not like ourselves, and as corporations become increasingly more diverse our brains constantly make snap judgments, either consciously or subconsciously. Each time this occurs, the seed of potential conflict is planted.

Many corporations believe that the most effective way to lead is to take all emotions out of business and strictly deal with facts. Although this is a widely held notion, it will never work because it requires humans to stop being human. Our emotions serve many functions, most particularly in helping coordinate and assign priorities to our brain patterns. It is impossible for humans to deny our emotions. Emotional capacities evolved along with our cognitive capacities. Without the ability to respond to stimuli with the appropriate emotions, critical decision-making becomes impossible.

This notion has been demonstrated through studies of patients with frontal lobe brain damage. These patients have a diminished capacity to respond emotionally and appropriately to stimuli that produced strong and proper reactions in people with undamaged brains. These particular patients were also afflicted with severe indecisiveness, making it impossible for them to plan their lives or make even the simplest decisions like what to eat for dinner. By their own accounts, the brains of these patients are flooded with information to help them make decisions, yet they simply are unable to do so. Although this may be an extreme example, it shows how critical one's emotions are in the decision-making process, and it indicates that without emotions, the best choice might not be made.

Clearly emotion should not be the primary decision-making factor; the human brain has evolved so that we can find a balance. Evolutionary psychology proposes that our minds are composed of mechanisms called psychological adaptations. These adaptations were favored by natural selection because they solved evolutionary problems faced by our ancestors. Examples of these mechanisms are things like mating strategies, cheater detection, status sensitivity, and language. It is clear to us that there are many programs that have been built into the brain by natural selection. In actuality, those programs are patterns of connection, and contain many well-tested assumptions about the physical and biological world surrounding us. The brain assumes things like the presence of gravity, spatial location while driving, and the unity of solid objects. These programs process sensory inputs and allow us to develop perceptions based on remarkably little information. Without consciously realizing it, our brains impose a structure on the world our eyes see. At this point in human evolution, our brains can calculate billions of bits of information in milliseconds to allow us to see and talk naturally and effortlessly.

Connections in our brains allow us to automatically do extremely difficult tasks, such as recognizing a friend's voice on the telephone. These same connections also allow us to walk, talk, eat, fight, sleep, pick up a fork, and put food in our mouths. Each activity is performed unconsciously; they have all become automatic to us only after millions of years of natural selection. Due to evolution, the neurons in our brain have learned to connect without a conscious effort. Despite these impressive feats, the genetic map does not possess specific instruction for dealing with every conceivable behavioral situation. Humans must often deal with these circumstances as they arise and make decisions using past experience, emotion, and even the subconscious.

Cognitive neuroscientist Benjamin Libet of the University of California conducted research on consciousness and free will. In his study, he asked participants to press a button whenever they wished and to also note the time at which they felt the impulse to press the button. Libet used electrodes to measure the mounting electrical tension as participants' brains prepared to initiate action. He assumed that the tension would build at the moment when his subjects felt the impulse to push the button. Surprisingly, Libet was wrong. He found that our brains prepare for action over one third of a second before we consciously decide to act. Although we go through life believing our decisions are made consciously, this experiment clearly suggests that something on a subconscious level also impels us toward our decisions.

Furthermore, at times the brain scrambles messages before they reach the conscious mind. It is not unreasonable to conjecture that our subconscious brains may tendentiously influence information about our social interactions, just as they direct sensory and motor information. This management of information makes self-deception possible. The interval between subconscious awareness and the conscious decision to act allows plenty of time for the unconscious to tinker with the information before it reaches consciousness. If we are to have any hope of truly understanding our minds and ourselves, we must use a combination of personal introspection and scientific investigation to better comprehend the complexities of our decision-making processes.

Do Our Brains Play Tricks on Us?

Neuroscientists Sandra Aamodt and Sam Wang understand that "the brain does not simply gather and stockpile information as a computer's hard drive does." Facts are first stored in the brain's hippocampus, a structure deep inside the brain about the size and shape of a curled pinkie finger. Each time we recall a fact, our brain "writes" it again, and during this recoding it is also reprocessed. Over time, the fact is gradually transferred to the cerebral cortex and is separated away from the context in which it was originally learned. For example, although you can remember Tokyo is the capital of Japan, you have probably forgotten how you learned that. This series of events is known as source amnesia and can also lead people to forget whether a statement is true or false. Even if a false statement is presented as such, people will often later remember it as true. With time, this misremembering gets worse. Even if we initially disbelieve a false statement, by the time it is reprocessed and moved from the hippocampus to the cerebral cortex, the brain may fail to sustain that disbelief and may store it as fact. When the source of the statement has been forgotten, the message and its implications gain strength.

As previously stated, humans are not consciously aware of the amount of work the brain does. Our perceptions are based not just on the external world, but also on the evolved characteristics and constraints of our nervous systems, so we tend to miss a great deal of what's around us. Our brains' capacity to scramble information, combined with certain genetic predispositions that have evolved over millions of years, means that they can play cognitive tricks on us. One example is a phenomenon called attention blindness, which occurs when humans focus on a task or point of view so closely that they miss the obvious. Consider a group of participants who are asked to view a video and count the number of times a basketball is passed between a team wearing black T-shirts and a team wearing white T-shirts. After watching the video, participants are asked if they saw anything else and the answer is primarily no. These individuals were so focused on counting that 90 percent of them missed a gorilla walking through the court and pounding its chest during the middle of the film. The participants' brains were so intently focused on completing one particular task—counting the number of passes—that they were unable to observe the entire scene.

Noted Stanford University biologist Paul Ehrlich also commented on the brain's functionality when he wrote, "Your brain helps to determine what you see. Turn your head rapidly from side to side, and you will perceive your head moving in a room that is stationary.... Now if you have a video camera, turn it on and move it around in the same way as you moved your head, and then play back the sequence. On the videotape, the room moves at a dizzying pace, and you may even feel a little seasick watching it." Ehrlich wondered what made the difference in that situation and found that our brains receive information from special sensor receptors that inform it of the position and movement of the parts of your body. The brain realizes your head is moving and is programmed to compensate for the movement to keep your mental representation of the environment stationary.

The brain works in many ways to recognize and organize the incoming visual data it receives. These ways are called gestalt laws, which refer to our senses' ability to create structure; in German, gestalt literally means "shape" or "figure." Gestalt focuses particularly on the visual recognition of figures and whole forms. This field of study has found that sometimes our brains will fill in the blanks to create a whole when only a fraction of a piece of information is before us. Although it may seem contradictory, our brains are also programmed to let us see what we expect to see; when several people are given the same information, they will often reach different conclusions. This is called selective perception. Our nervous systems help construct the reality we believe in, and the characteristics of those systems unquestionably bias that reality, ultimately affecting our behaviors and natures. An exercise we use in seminars depicts the inefficiencies of our brains and the fact that our eyes can distort what we see. Participants are asked to view pictures of two boxes, and the vast majority of the participants see the boxes very differently. Most see one rectangle and one square, but the reality is that they are exactly the same size; they are both rectangles.

Another trick our brains play is made apparent in our tendencies to dichotomize the world without any gradations. Almost from birth we must decide: good or bad, friend or foe, right or wrong, big or small, freewill or determinism, mind or body. Dichotomizing can be extremely useful when quick decisions are needed in order to stay alive, but that is rarely the situation in today's world. The decisions we must make in our lives today require much more complex and slower processes of thinking. After one realizes this, it is easy to see why humans have difficulty being objective, and why conflict occurs when people with implicit and explicit biases and stereotypes are brought together.

What Did We Learn? A Summary

1. Genes and environments work together to create an individual's mindset. It is impossible to determine which one has more influence on human beings, at least until further scientific developments shed more light on this issue.

2. Throughout history our brains have developed patterns that remain a part of our genetic makeup because they have helped ensure our survival. As a result, we have developed perceptions based on these patterns, some of which are unconscious, while others are conscious.

3. Our emotions play a crucial role in prioritizing and assigning reactions. It is important that we understand that we cannot make decisions without these emotions.

4. Biological evolution has given the brain certain predispositions, which can be modified by environmental influences.

5. The good news is that we can continually update all mental programs on the basis of our experience. The brain has predispositions, but in most situations the brain realizes that the environmental information of the moment is a better guide upon which to base our actions than the evolutionary past.

CHAPTER 4

Stereotyping is Human but Extremely Dangerous—How Explicit and Implicit Biases and Stereotypes Impact Human Interactions

"We may have different religions, different languages, different colored skin, but we all belong to one human race."

– Kofi Annan

In today's world, almost everything we need is literally at our fingertips; through the simple strokes of a keyboard, we have easier access to more information than ever before. It is clear that the information age has changed our world in innumerable ways. We now live in a world united by human experiences, and we routinely see people who look and act differently from us, whether on the Internet, the television, in print, or in person. Our rapidly changing world can be difficult to navigate, but we should recognize that it also offers opportunities to learn about different kinds of people, and to understand why they are the way they are.

Most countries maintain constitutions and laws that uphold the concepts of fairness, equality, and non-discrimination. Many of us have also received education about discrimination and biases; we profess to know right from wrong, what is legal and illegal. We profess to be gender and color blind, to love most religions, appreciate most cultures, accept skinny and fat people, gays and straights, rich and poor, and so on. And yet despite these assertions, implicit and explicit biases and stereotypes still exist, and as a direct result, discriminatory behaviors still occur in our personal and professional lives. Why?

Most basically, our brains are programmed to collect and store data that we call upon automatically and unconsciously. On top of this, as humans have evolved we have consciously created stereotypes and biases. The underlying reason for many of these developments stems from the desire by one cultural group to minimize and ultimately eliminate the competition from another cultural group, a tool developed during early human history to ensure survival.

Stereotypes and Biases—Cognitive Tools or Cultural Weapons?

Although a person's biases and stereotypes depend on their own unique experiences, at ARMC Global we define concepts like racism, sexism, ethnocentrism, and homophobia as cultural ideologies that characterize the dominant group as being inherently superior to non-dominant groups. People in dominant or in-power groups, through societal institutions, develop, spread, and enforce the myths and stereotypes that are the foundation for their dominant social, economic, and political position. These views become ingrained in the minds not only of the oppressors but also of the oppressed.

Concepts like racism and sexism are cultural. For example, males from certain cultures are more likely than males from other cultures to consider themselves superior to women. However, we can find examples of stereotyped or biased thought in nearly every culture, in all parts of the world: many Japanese citizens perceive Koreans as inferior to them; some light-skinned people from countries such as Brazil, India, and China believe they are superior to the darker skinned people; in Northern Ireland there are still great divides between those of different religions; many men in Middle Eastern countries like Saudi Arabia believe women to be inferior and in a surprising number of societies this inferiority is still formalized by the legal system; and Black males in the United States are still perceived as dangerous by the mainstream, predominantly White society, and even by some Blacks, as the Trayvon Martin case illustrated. If stereotypes are not challenged, they can quickly become widespread beliefs, eventually turning into society's norms.

Another unfortunate trend found throughout the world is that the people who believe and adhere to these types of thoughts are often in positions of power and are thus able to develop and enforce the stereotypes that serve as the foundation for their positions of authority in the first place. Often these negativities are not necessarily a matter of personal

beliefs or attitudes, but rather accessory expressions of insti-
tutionalized patterns within social, economic, religious, and
political systems. Whether personal or not, these beliefs
have been used to maintain and justify the elite's social,
economic, and political positions, which have also become
rooted deeply in the structure and fabric of our societies.

The power struggle between dominant groups who
seek to maintain their positions and the outside groups
who seek to change the status quo stands at the center of
the problems we face today. The fear of losing dominance
drives these groups, whether consciously or unconsciously,
to nurture myths and stereotypes about the outside groups.
When looked at carefully, displays of bias are simply defense
mechanisms most often used by the dominant to deal with
their own insecurities. These mindsets can be changed, but
if they are not, the oppressed groups also start to believe
these stereotypes, which compound their psychological
stresses. By accepting and internalizing racist, sexist, religious, fascist, homophobic, and ethnocentric assumptions,
the oppressed groups can explain and justify their subordinate societal position, making it even harder for them to
break through these constructed barriers. This dynamic
plays out in much of the world today.

While racism, sexism, extreme ethnocentrism, homophobia, and religious intolerance fragment groups within a
nation, xenophobia can bind a country's major ethnic groups
together through fear and hatred of all things foreign.
According to sociologist Wilhelm Heitmeyer of Bielefeld
University in Germany, "Hostility to foreigners should be
understood not primarily as a personality characteristic, but
rather as a social and political 'tidal current' whose ebb and

flow can be influenced politically and limited by the action of social groups and governmental authorities and their definitions of violence." Yet many people do not view our current political leanings toward xenophobia as negative. For example, some consider the American Tea Party a valid and important political organization, but further examination reveals it should be more accurately classified as a xenophobic movement in the United States. It seems to have an insidious implicit bias against non-Whites, immigrants, non-Christians, LGBT individuals, and anyone they perceive as "un-American." These kinds of ideologies are not exclusive to the United States. In Moscow, young Russian males have taken to attacking people who look physically non-Russian in attempts to "preserve" their country. Additionally, the Chinese minority population of Malaysia, many of whom are often financially successful, is often scapegoated for their country's difficult economic situations, and at times even brutally attacked. Finally, even Israel, surrounded by enemies and characterized by centuries of oppression, can turn on those who are considered different, as the recent attacks on dark-skinned and immigrant Jews attest.

These types of xenophobia contribute to nationalism and isolationism. The ideas inspire and justify bloody ethnic and religious struggles, as well as unfair immigration laws. The degree and extent of xenophobia in a country often parallels its economic and social status. As economies slow down, as traditional social networks break down, and as the nature of cultures change as a result of ongoing and rapid globalization, xenophobia increases. Instead of accepting and adapting to these changes and challenges, many cultures look for a scapegoat, and they find one in "the other." A society often convinces itself that minorities, foreigners, nonbelievers, and "alien" cultures are destroying the old order, ruining the economy, or compromising the traditional way of life. While it is true that many oppressed groups internalize and believe in these negative impressions, we can also see that some respond with hatred and violence.

While hatred and violence should never be tolerated, it is possible to trace the reasoning behind this reaction, and the ultimate cycle of stereotyping that it creates. In the face of a dominant majority, those who are oppressed and excluded often feel powerless; despite attempts at contributing to or uniting with society, they are often deemed unfit. Their social status is threatened and their innate sense of competition reminds them of the potential effects of such threats: isolation and estrangement. With few alternatives, violence becomes a subjectively expressive means (or even an end in itself), for it creates clarity in unclear situations.

Further compounding this dynamic is the disconnected nature of modern life and the breaking down of family structures and kin groups. Opportunistic, morally bankrupt politicians, religious leaders, and business leaders have fanned the latent fires of xenophobia throughout the world. Heitmeyer and other social scientists believe that many countries are susceptible to these trends because of increases in freedom and mobility and a weakening of family ties. And so, while entire groups of people are programmed to distrust or exclude other groups of people, it is the individual alone who must bear the risks of failure. When we analyze this information it becomes clear how the cycles of hatred, violence, and discrimination are perpetuated.

The Natural Tendency to Stereotype

With all the economic, technical, and scientific progress humans have made, why do we still rely on stereotyping rather than objective rationality? One of the answers to this question is literally hundreds of thousands of years old. As explained earlier, the human brain does not have the capacity to start from scratch to analyze the billions of bits of information that bombard our minds daily. Thus, the brain has a "rapid response team" that allows us to quickly assess and make sense out of a complex, unclear, and at times confusing world. Without this ability, humans would not have been able to survive in a wild and largely unpredictable world, where hesitating for a second could have meant the difference between life and death.

Now the downside: there are many examples in which high rates of speed lead to a reduction in accuracy. Take, for instance, rushing through a complicated financial report, driving too quickly on a curved road, or trying to say a tongue twister five times rapidly. Our instinctive fight, freeze, or flight rapid response team is no different. The result is less accurate perceptions and conclusions. We are prone to error or noise in the system and our quick calculations and subsequent classifications of information may tend to oversimplify reality.

To compound this problem, our brains may have needed this survival mechanism in the earlier, harsher environments that humans navigated, but it is overused in today's modern and less brutal world. Although we differ socially, politically, technologically, and economically from our ancient forebears, our brains have not evolved as rapidly.

We retain our flawed thought processes that were derived from a survival instinct that was crucial tens of thousands of years ago but outdated today. These circumstances are not ideal, but recognition of these tendencies will allow us to overcome the detrimental effects of snap decisions, many of which are based on stereotypes and biases.

The Myth of Objectivity

Most people understand that stereotypes are not socially acceptable and therefore will not easily admit to having them. And yet, if there is no recognition and acceptance of this very human tendency, then there really can be no true progress toward overcoming it. There are many steps we can take to change our behavior, and most require an open mind. For example, in those societies that pride themselves on fairness and equality, most people claim that they judge others according to their character, skill, performance, or merit. But we should recognize that such terms as character, skill, performance, and merit are defined differently by various societies and by each of us as human beings.

In addition to keeping an open mind, it is important to recognize the difficulty in being truly objective. Research has shown that most individuals grossly overestimate their ability to be objective, not only because it is a human tendency to do so, but also because the corporate world and societies have perpetuated this myth about human objectivity. ARMC Global has conducted research that clearly demonstrates our lack of objectivity. We asked thousands of participants from around the world to use a few words to characterize "types" of people based on their knowledge and experience. Here are just a few examples of the terms they used:

Jews

- Money and power
- Hard workers
- Business minded
- Family oriente
- Thrifty
- Sad history
- Ancient tradition
- God's chosen people
- Rich/wealthy
- Religious
- Opportunists
- Big nose
- Cheap
- Whining

The French

- Artistic/art
- Thin
- Sexual
- Romantic
- Slow
- Hate Americans
- Wine, make great wine, like wine
- Food, cuisine
- Love the people, love the country
- Fashion, stylish
- Culture, great art and museums
- Arrogant
- Rude
- Have an attitude

Women

- Nurturing
- Beautiful
- Pampered
- Emotional
- Intuitive
- Strong
- Companion
- Talkative

- Multi-tasker
- Smart/intelligent
- Powerful/have power
- Worry unnecessarily about their weight
- Stubborn
- Manipulative
- Terrible drivers
- Rock

- Perceived below men
- Underestimated
- Love them
- Can do it all
- Sexy, beautiful
- Ambitious
- Smell good
- Strong sex
- Greatly undervalued

Hispanics/Latinos

- Many kids
- Touchy
- Beautiful people
- Resourceful
- Lazy
- Culturally rich
- Hard workers
- Smelly
- Poor, discriminated against

- Are everywhere
- Loud
- Under-educated
- Arrogant
- Big on family
- Delicious food
- Gangs
- Drugs

Chinese

- Very focused
- Not inclusive
- Smart
- Thrifty
- Communist
- Mysterious

- Family oriented
- Culture with deep tradition
- Hard workers
- Powerful
- Lucky

- Respectful
- Can't tell the difference from Japanese
- Smelly
- Xenophobic
- Disciplined
- Innovative
- Capable
- Food, shrimp fried rice
- Sushi

People who seek mental health assistance

- Big problems
- Grave
- Unstable
- Honorable and thoughtful
- Pain, depression, medicine
- Smart, self-aware
- Don't understand
- Have something broken
- Common
- Courageous
- Realistic
- Smart
- Confused
- Overwhelmed

Politicians

- Thick skin
- Men
- White shirts, polished
- Work hard
- Career focused
- Dishonest
- Hidden agenda
- Distrust, don't trust
- Sneaky, slick
- Opportunists
- Hypocritical
- Cheat
- Crooks
- Self-serving
- Self-important
- Full of s…
- Good speakers
- Good people
- Good intentions
- Liars/lie, dishonest

- Corrupt
- Egotistical
- Stuffy
- Incompetent

People who are overweight

- Low self-esteem
- Great sense of humor, funny
- Undisciplined
- Unhealthy
- Struggling
- Lazy
- Want to lose weight
- Sensitive
- Misunderstood
- Eat too much
- Careless
- Unhappy with themselves
- Hard life
- Sad
- Angry
- Emotional

Brazilians

- Colorful
- Sexy
- Easy-going
- Soccer
- Music
- Beaches, suntan
- Portuguese
- Tolerant
- Good looking
- Hard workers
- Enjoy life, party
- Tolerant
- Promiscuous, risqué
- Fake/plastic surgery
- Exotic
- Wild
- Trouble
- Irresponsible
- Proud
- Don't wear many clothes

South Africans

- Mandela
- Soccer
- Prejudice
- Apartheid, racial
- Beautiful country
- Music, life
- Romantic
- Accents
- Great
- Whites still control
- Poor
- Friends
- Diamonds, World Cup
- Culture, dark

Nigerians

- Colored
- Good sales people
- Would like to meet more
- Friend
- Smart
- Scams/email scams
- Violent
- Constantly at war
- Misgoverned
- Rip-off artist
- Religious violence
- High values

East Indian Asians

- Food
- Technology/ computer
- Smart/intelligent
- Driven
- Misunderstood
- Smelly
- All look alike
- Not trustworthy
- Difficult to under- stand, strong accent
- Exotic
- Mongolia, India
- Indian food, slum dog
- Smart, doctors

Muslims

- Practice religion regularly
- Misunderstood
- Secretive
- Lack of equality for women
- Could be terrorists
- Religious zealots
- High morals
- Not friendly
- Disciplined
- Koran, prayer
- Just like everyone else
- Scary
- Terrorists
- Brainwashed, confused
- Make me nervous
- Wrongly accused

Clearly humans are not objective thinkers; we approach each person we encounter with a set of ideas that we have developed through experience, knowledge, hearsay, media portrayals, and taught behaviors. For an example of how these factors can impact our decision-making processes, consider the following promotion scenario. In a corporation, the managers are ready to make promotions and have a group of qualified candidates. Although they are aware of the consequences for discrimination, these managers also have implicit biases and stereotypes that affect their decision-making. The candidates are all qualified, so the personal preferences of the managers are often the deciding factor in the end. One candidate speaks with an accent, one has a different ethnic background from the manager, one is of a different race, another is of a different age, and one attended the manager's alma mater. Who ends up getting the promotion? Research shows that those managers will be more likely to choose candidates who are most like them, playing into the in-group favoritism that humans developed for survival reasons nearly one hundred thousand years ago.

Overcoming Our Stereotypes and Biases

Implicit assumptions about those who are different from us affect our perceptions of their abilities, particularly if we do not understand or acknowledge that these assumptions arise from within ourselves. To better understand where our biases and stereotypes come from, it is helpful to remember that there are two types of biases: explicit and implicit. Our explicit views and perceptions are those of which we are aware and can control. We employ them intentionally as the result of introspection, deep thought, and closely examined beliefs. They are also the attitudes and judgments we are willing to endorse, support, and consciously act upon. These biases are formed not only from our experiences and socialization, but also by societal values, beliefs, and behaviors.

By contrast, our implicit assumptions are those that we do not know exist and cannot control without considerable work and self-examination. These biases and stereotypes are not a result of intentional thought and have not been subjected to any introspection. Because we are not aware of their existence and do not claim these beliefs, we cannot endorse or support them. It is this subterranean pull, which makes implicit assumptions so very dangerous. These unexamined beliefs prevent even the most well-meaning humans from making truly unbiased decisions.

We all tend to favor those who are most like us, but at what cost? How we define our allies can vary greatly based on our life experiences. Are we sacrificing the originality, the creativity, the problem solving, and the higher levels of performance that Proactive Inclusion® brings for the sake of comfort and the known? Are we forsaking relationships with people who are different from us, not based on character and positive values but on superficial appearance?

It is clear that there is only one way to overcome this tendency to bias and stereotype—we must each understand our own life experiences and values to understand our particular explicit and implicit assumptions. We must understand how the human brain works on some level—its shortcomings, its strengths, and its weaknesses. We must work extremely hard to not stereotype and show bias. This is not an indictment of human nature; this is simply a realization that we all have our own work to do before we are able to act as objectively as possible. Before we can truly create an environment based on Trust, Respect, Empathy, and Ethics (GlobalTREE^SM), before we can truly appreciate, value, respect, and harness the talents, creativity, and experiences of all employees, and, yes, before we can move toward much fairer organizations and societies, we must acknowledge and understand how implicit biases and stereotypes interfere with achieving these objectives.

Supporting Data for Skeptics

Led by Dr. Mahzarin Banaji of Harvard University, researchers from Harvard, University of Virginia, and University of Washington have created an online test to assess biases and stereotypes on a variety of topics like skin color, gender, religion, and age. Millions of people from a number of different countries have taken the Implicit Association Test (IAT) and the results show that no race, ethnic group, gender, or culture can escape favoritism or the human tendency to stereotype.

ARMCG used Harvard's IAT to assess the biases and stereotypes in the organizations where we have consulted. In one company we found that 69 percent of the managers and leaders had a moderate to strong preference for light skin tone. In another company we found that 68 percent of women and 78 percent of men associate men with careers and women with family.

Dr. Banaji and many researchers around the world also study the pervasiveness of implicit and explicit stereotypes and biases and the variety of areas in which they occur. What follows is a compilation of their studies:

Implicit vs. Explicit Biases

- Data gathered from Harvard's online IAT over a span of several years show that although few participants report conscious bias against African-Americans, Arabs, Jews, gays, or the poor, participants have substantial implicit biases against these groups.
- Researchers Do-Yeong Kim and Hye-Jung Oh conducted a study in 2001 that found that South and North Koreans have significant unfavorable implicit biases toward one another, despite their indication in various bias tests of no form of prejudices toward one another.

The Nature of Biases and Stereotypes

- Studies on implicit and explicit tests found that results can be manipulated. Participants are able to change their responses according to their goals and intentions. Responses may also differ according to the situation presented. We can infer that individuals have some control over their implicit and explicit assumptions, but only depending on their personal motivations and the context.

- A study on stereotyping and self-worth conducted by researchers at University of Surrey and University of London compared African-Caribbean students to Caucasian students. African-Caribbean children with higher self-worth stereotyped people of color more than African-Caribbean children with lower self-worth. Conversely, Caucasian children with higher self-worth stereotyped people of color less than Caucasian children with lower self-worth.

- A study published in the Journal of Personality and Social Psychology tested the hypothesis that a contextual change would have an effect on automatic stereotypes. All participants were exposed to a Chinese woman, and stereotypes of both Chinese people and women were measured. In one depiction the woman was applying makeup and in another, she was using chopsticks. Those who viewed the makeup scenario reported more stereotypic ideas of women and fewer traits stereotypic of Chinese people. The participants who saw the woman using chop-sticks responded with stronger responses to Chinese stereotypes.

- Research conducted by Steven J. Spencer of Waterloo University and his colleagues revealed that the preservation of one's self-image is a powerful motivator. It was found that a threat to self-image would motivate the person to invoke negative stereotypes of others. Therefore, a person may inhibit these negative stereotypes and activate positive ones when doing so would be beneficial.

- In a study conducted by researchers at Dartmouth University and Harvard University, the participants who were assigned to a role of superiority displayed a greater level of automatic prejudice toward those below them than those participants assigned to an equal-status role. Participants who were placed in the most subordinate role exhibited the least amount of automatic prejudice.

Bias in Action

- A Rutgers University study examined the connection between implicit biases of Jews, Asians, and Blacks and the impact these unconscious biases would have on their ability to objectively evaluate proposals. Students were asked to examine a budget proposal and then make recommendations for allocating funding to specific student organizations. Those who exhibited greater implicit bias against Jewish, Asian, or Black individuals tended to recommend budgets that discriminated more against organizations devoted those particular groups' interests.

- A study published in the *Journal of General Internal Medicine*, conducted by a team of researchers including Dr. Banaji, examined the responses of 287 physicians who were shown a photograph and brief clinical vignette of a middle-aged patient who came to the hospital with symptoms of acute coronary syndrome. In some cases the patient was Black and in other cases the patient was White. Most physicians did not acknowledge conscious bias, but on average showed a moderate to large implicit anti-Black bias. The greater a physician's racial bias, the less likely he or she was to give efficient and effective treatment to the Black patient versus the White patient.

- The University of Kalmar in Sweden sent corporations job applications with the exact same education, work experience, and skill level on behalf of fictional male candidates with either Arab, Muslim, or Swedish names. After tracking the 193 human resources professionals who had evaluated the applications, the researchers at University of Kalmar discovered that the greater the employer's bias, the less likely it was that an applicant with an Arab name would be called for an interview.

Group Biases and Stereotypes

The following studies outline the different types of biases and stereotypes that people have about certain groups and categories of people. This list does not encompass all types of bias and stereotype.

Biases and stereotypes based on gender:

- A group of researchers from Harvard, MIT, Berkeley, Calcutta, and the International Monetary Fund studied voter attitudes toward female leaders in Indian villages. In villages that did not have female leaders, the results found voters to be biased against female leaders, but less so with more exposure. Voters, particularly men, rated leadership speeches more negatively when the speaker's voice was female. However, this bias was absent in other villages that currently had a female leader. Females had less voter bias against women than males had initially, and those opinions were unaffected when exposure was considered.

- According to experiments conducted at Lawrence University, individuals who held a stronger implicit bias toward women were less likely to select a qualified woman who exhibited stereotypically masculine qualities for a job requiring stereotypically feminine qualities. The participants' perceptions were that the woman was less socially skilled than a man, despite having the same qualifications.

Biases and stereotypes based on weight:

- In a University of Virginia study that surveyed biases against overweight people, all weight groups indicated significant anti-overweight biases and stereotypes on implicit tests, regardless of the responder's weight. Thinner people displayed significantly more negative stereotypes against overweight people than obese people displayed.

- One study headed by researchers at Yale University revealed that medical and health professionals who work with obese people negatively stigmatize their own patients. Physicians associated obesity with poor hygiene, laziness, dishonesty, and lack of commitment. Nurses perceived their patients as overindulgent, lazy, full of unresolved anger, and unsuccessful.

Biases and stereotypes based on race:

- In a study on discrimination in resumes published by the National Bureau of Economic Research, applicants had the same experience, education, and skills; the only difference was the names. Those resumes with White-sounding names were 50 percent more likely to be called for interviews than those with Black-sounding names.

- Kenneth Clark's landmark study conducted more than fifty years ago used five-year-old girls and was replicated in 2009 showing similarly disturbing results. When given the option, 70 percent of the young Black girls in the study selected a White doll over a Black doll saying she looked nicer and the other doll looked bad. It should be noted that in all studies ARMCG has reviewed, white children prefer white skin over black skin by huge margins.

- Harvard's online IAT data show that African-Americans report a strong explicit preference for their group but show relatively less implicit preference, while White Americans report a lower explicit bias and higher implicit bias for their group.

- Ohio State University psychologist Will A. Cunningham measured White people's brain activity as they viewed a series of White and Black faces. His team found the Black faces they flashed for only 30 milliseconds triggered greater activity in the amygdala, a brain area associated with vigilance and sometimes fear. The effect was most pronounced among people who demonstrated strong implicit racial bias. Provocatively, the same study revealed that when the same faces were shown for half a second, they elicited heightened activity in prefrontal brain areas associated with detecting internal conflicts and controlling responses. These results hinted that individuals were consciously trying to suppress their implicit negative associations.

Biases and stereotypes based on beauty:

- Another study conducted by and shown on ABC found that at the age of five, children had already developed a stereotype painting attractive people as more cooperative, competent, and likable than average-looking people. The same study revealed that attractive women tend to get more job offers and higher salaries than equally qualified, less attractive candidates. Also, children prefer attractive teachers even when less attractive counterparts are kinder and more attentive.

Biases and stereotypes based on skin color:

- A new study from Vanderbilt University found that immigrants in the United States with a lighter skin tone make more money than those with darker skin. This remained true when considering other diverse characteristics such as language proficiency, work experience, and education that might affect wages. Immigrants with the lightest skin color were found to earn 8–15 percent more than those with the darkest skin color. The effects of skin color were also apparent among individuals with the same ethnicity, race, or country of origin.
- In Italy, psychologist Luigi Castelli of the University of Padova examined the racial attitudes and behaviors of seventy-two White Italian

families and found that young children's racial preferences were unaffected by their parents' explicit racial attitudes. However, children whose mothers had greater negative implicit attitudes toward Blacks tended to choose a White playmate over a Black one and ascribed more negative traits to a fictional Black child than to a fictional White child. Children whose mothers showed less implicit racial bias were less likely to exhibit racial preferences.

- Multiple studies show the biases Hispanics have against other Hispanics based on skin color. One study published in *Social Cognition* revealed American Hispanics and Chileans expressing strong preference for lighter skinned Hispanics over darker skinned Hispanics. While American Hispanics do not show preferences for Whites over Hispanics, Chilean participants preferred Whites to lighter skinned Hispanics.

- Studies have demonstrated that both Whites and Blacks prefer a light-skinned Black to a dark-skinned Black. This type of bias was demonstrated in a study by psychology professor Matthew S. Harrison at the University of Georgia. Harrion's research found that a lighter skinned Black male with a bachelor's degree and typical work experience will still be preferred over a darker skinned Black male possessing an MBA and multiple past managerial positions.

Biases and stereotypes based on age:

- In analyzing the results of three years of responses from Harvard's online IAT, Dr. Banaji and her colleagues found that implicit age bias does not vary depending on the respondent's age. Both older and younger participants tend to have negative implicit attitudes toward the elderly and positive implicit attitudes toward the young. Conversely, there is an increase in explicit positive attitude toward the elderly as the age of the respondent increases.

What Humans and Organizations Can Do about Human Subjectivity

After reading the previous data, it is important to begin overcoming these tendencies. We must acknowledge that we are not completely objective or rational people. Stereotyping is normal, but it is extremely dangerous. It inevitably leads to misinterpretations, unresolved conflicts, and organizational ineffectiveness. Although the brain naturally stereotypes, we have the control to acknowledge and do something about this fact. Humans must recognize that constantly working on our subjectivity allows us to overcome stereotypes in order to develop organizations and societies that are based on Trust, Respect, Empathy, and Ethics (GlobalTREE^{SM}). A number of crucial issues were presented in the last few chapters. The following is an overview of the more salient points:

- We all make snap decisions and judgments in milliseconds, as a result of survival instincts that were developed hundreds of thousands of years ago. Although we have changed a great deal from the ancient peoples who relied on those instincts for survival, we still react the same way when faced with something or someone that is different or unknown.
- Our brains can play cognitive tricks on us, which complicates the matter of making snap decisions. For example, attention blindness is the process of being so focused on a particular object or task that we miss the obvious and distort the big picture.
- Our explicit views and perceptions are those of which we are aware and can control. They occur intentionally and may be the result of introspection and closely examined beliefs.
- Our implicit assumptions are those of which we are unaware, and therefore cannot control without considerable effort. And even then we might not be aware of them all the time. Because we are not aware of their existence, and, in many cases, do not consciously claim these beliefs, we do not endorse or support them. It is this very quality, their subconscious nature, that makes implicit assumptions so dangerous and detrimental to building relationships based on trust, respect, empathy, and ethics.

- The prevalence of biases and stereotypes suggests that even the most well-meaning person unwittingly allows unconscious thoughts and feelings to influence what should be objective decisions.
- People routinely change their memories to fit their beliefs, and what we remember depends very much on our biases.
- Even if we have absolutely no explicit biases, we are influenced by our expectations. What image comes to our minds when we think of a doctor, a nurse, a truck driver, or a terrorist?
- The way the human brain functions impacts our ability to see things accurately. At times there is a disparity between what the conscious mind does not observe and what the unconscious mind registers. Unless we are aware of this discrepancy we will not understand the effects it has on our behaviors.
- People have a tendency to give preferential treatment to those people who are most like themselves. This is done on an unconscious level, not only due to our human evolution to favor our kin or family group for survival, but also because of the existence of implicit biases and stereotypes.
- Biases are not dichotomous; we cannot divide people as "those who have biases" and "those who do not."

- If a person has a moderate bias and is aware of it, he or she will often be fairer than someone who has a slight bias and is not aware of it.
- Stereotypes and biases are instinctive and require a conscious effort to overcome; however, the mere conscious desire not to be biased cannot fully neutralize all bias.

The following are some very simple and practical actions that individuals can take in order to minimize their biases and promote healthy environments:

- Reflect on life experiences and significant emotional events that have shaped your value system, beliefs, and attitudes about those who are different from you. Answer relevant questions about where and when your influences were developed and shaped.
- Broaden your perspective on what affects those values and beliefs. Recognize that these are not only influenced by race, ethnicity, and gender, but also by language, age, education, religion, socioeconomic status, and sexual orientation, among other elements.
- Enroll in classes that examine and discuss cultures, values, and beliefs. Seek education on how the brain works and on biological and cultural evolution.
- Study another language; learn as many as you can.

- Learn as much as you can about your own culture from others within it.
- Request feedback from multiple sources about your strengths and weaknesses. In particular, try to get this from people of a different race, gender, class, religion, culture, etc.
- Seek out experiences that will enable you to practice your strengths and strengthen your weaknesses.
- Develop friendships and relationships with as many people from as many diverse backgrounds as you can, not only at work but outside of work as well.
- Join a board or community organization that focuses on a population different than your own.
- Listen closely to the views of people who are different from you and work hard to understand them, especially if these worldviews vary widely from your own.
- Volunteer to assist friends and acquaintances of other racial, ethnic, religious, gender, or class groups in their activities.
- Join organizations that expressly seek to advance the interests of people different from you.
- Make the decision to visit, socialize, or live in a community that has a lot of diversity and differs from your background or upbringing.
- Go to the Harvard Implicit Association website and take tests that measure your implicit biases and stereotypes. Learn and grow from the results of these tests.

- Take stereotyping exercises, such as the Opinion Survey, that analyze the thoughts that first come to mind when we hear certain phrases.
- Request feedback from multiple sources about your strengths and weaknesses related to diversity, Proactive Inclusion®, and GlobalTREE℠.
- Change whatever you can about yourself and be aware of the consequences if you do not.

It is very clear that considerable work must be done in order to minimize conflicts created by human subjectivities. These conflicts get in the way of organizations and societies fully utilizing all types of people and ideas. It becomes more obvious each day that for organizations and societies to function and prosper in this diverse and interconnected world, more resources have to be dedicated to this effort. While some leaders will say this is all "soft stuff," it is clear that if we do not deal with these issues immediately, conflict and inefficiency will be allowed to increase, essentially damaging working environments and societies beyond repair.

CHAPTER 5

The Complexity and Subjectivity of Human Cultures

"In the world of values, nature in itself is neutral...It is we who create value and our desires which confer value.... It is for us to determine the good life, not for nature."

– Bertrand Russell

Thus far, we have explored human nature, discussed the various shortcomings of the human brain, and examined the reasons behind biases and stereotypes. These factors play a crucial role in the cultural conflicts that exist in organizations and societies and lead to dysfunctional behaviors, inefficiencies, and distrust of others. One of the greatest challenges facing leaders is the ability to constructively manage the numerous and extremely diverse cultures within their companies. Adding to that challenge is the fact that inside those cultures are individuals who are entirely unique. Despite these differences, companies still need to be able to communicate and function reasonably well in order to survive. At ARMCG we propose using the fundamental tenets that exist across the scope of human experience, such as the desire for love, safety, respect, and good health, in order to make connections between people and achieve an environment in which all are valued.

As human societies evolved, we joined together to better protect and provide for our families and ourselves. Despite this need for unity, there have been clashes among different cultures throughout history in every part of the world. Fortunately, many of these conflicts have been resolved peacefully, but some have ended in violence and subjugation. In corporations, employees do not often use physical violence against their colleagues, but they behave destructively by undermining, lying, backstabbing, and withholding important information, creating an environment that damages corporations emotionally and financially.

The first step to begin minimizing these disputes and dealing with the diversity of our interconnected world is to create proactively inclusive environments based on Trust, Respect, Empathy, and Ethics (GlobalTREE[SM]), as outlined in Chapter Two. Obviously, this is no easy task. As the data ARMCG collected from thousands of employees over the past fifteen years suggest, there is a tremendous amount of work to be done. Illustrative of this point are the responses to a survey we conducted using ten international business units. Participants were asked to rate their level of agreement with the following statements, 1 being "to no extent" and 10 being "to a great extent." The numbers below are the average of the responses from thousands of managers.

Senior leaders and employees display keen global awareness of the market(s) in which they work, including their customers' cultural needs, values, and expectations. – 6.5

The company has built trusting and respectful relationships with key stakeholders in all countries where it does business. – 6.5

Cultural conflict styles are not ignored and solutions for effective interactions are developed. – 5.3

A systematic strategy has been developed to assist employees in understanding, appreciating, and valuing cultural and language differences. – 4.4

From this data, it is clear that although these issues are being addressed, scores need to improve. A great deal of systematic work is needed to prepare leaders and employees to understand and effectively deal with the issues surrounding a diverse environment. To begin, we must always keep in mind that humans essentially evolved from the same species, family, and location. Our primary and greatest difference is not what is skin deep, but what is within our minds—humans have created these differences, whether real or imagined. At our most basic level, humans typically desire love, respect, trust, appreciation, understanding, and fair treatment. We also want and need to be a productive part of families, organizations, and societies. Emotionally, we care for and protect our loved ones, and most of us feel great sympathy when we see others suffering. It is in these basic human qualities that most of us can find common ground with others to build Trust, Respect, Empathy, and Ethics (GlobalTREE[SM]), regardless of cultural differences.

What Is Culture?

While reading the term "culture" throughout this book, each individual has inevitably applied his or her own definition to it, whether consciously or subconsciously. Before continuing, it is important to define the word for the specific purposes of this book. Considering there are as many different ways to define culture as there are people willing to write about it, I reduce the definition to three simple but important ideas. Culture is the network of values, beliefs, and assumptions on which we base our behaviors. Human culture is the product of learning, particularly from experiences with people and societal institutions. Societies have created their unique cultures by developing workable solutions to the problems they face living in their own environments. Within a society's culture are the specific social and familial structures, religions, political and economic systems, clothing, cuisine, art, music, and laws, all of which are determined by such factors as population density, geography, climate, agriculture, animals, language, history, and neighboring cultures.

An individual's values are the broad tendencies to prefer certain ideals to others. Explicit values are internalized beliefs regarding what is right, good, and ethical. Humans believe their own values to be proper, appropriate, and often indisputable. These individual ideas take form mostly because of various socially defined factors. These factors can include generational beliefs, socioeconomic status, education, religion, immigration status, racial identity, political affiliation, gender, age, sexual orientation, or disability status. Individual values, beliefs, and assumptions can vary greatly, but when viewed on a collective level they coalesce and define correct and incorrect behavior for the group. Within cultural groups, the values held by the majority then become social norms. Despite these supposedly "normal" sets of guidelines, the rules and conventions of a society are not necessarily understood or appreciated by those who do not belong to it. Even individuals within a society will have a wide range of interpretations and commitment to adherence to their norms. Further compounding this dynamic is the fact that cultures today are constantly overlapping and influencing one another.

It is clear that humanity is undergoing a process of cultural homogenization. One of the largest factors in this phenomenon is mass media. For the first several decades of modern communications, most of the television, cinema, and electronic programming viewed around the world originated in Western nations. However, due primarily to the proliferation of the Internet over the past twenty years, media culture now flows in and from many directions. As a result, cultural traits from all over the world have circulated widely, connecting societies that only years ago had little knowledge of each other. For example, hip-hop music has become increasingly popular among Palestinian youth in Gaza; the influence of Japanese *animé* is easily identified in American cartoons; Jamaican dancehall music has found its way to electronic music venues across the European continent; Latin American *telenovelas* are watched all over the world. Along with the spread of media, the Internet, social networking, inexpensive travel, and increased global trade have made it easier for people to migrate, further blurring the boundaries of culture.

Why Is Culture Irrational?

Geert Hofstede, who has conducted landmark research in the field of culture and its impact on organization dynamics, defines culture as "the collective programming of the mind distinguishing the members of one group or category of people from another." Each person's specific DNA makes that individual's mental programming unique; however, we also know that cultural norms often level that individuality. Contrary to what many think, humans are not born with completely blank slates. Every person has a unique genetic makeup, and although at birth there are a few blank spots, society quickly fills them in. Babies begin life with a very simple sense of kinship to all other humans; there is no concept of race, gender, ethnicity, religion, or class. The only thing that matters is that they are cared for, fed, and loved. Most infants and young children are open and comfortable with any person who shows them love. These little human beings are genetically programmed so that adults will want to care for them. With their fascinating and adorable manner, they convince us to attend to their extreme and constant needs...at least for the first ten years of their lives, and in many cases beyond.

Children learn racism, sexism, homophobia, religious intolerance, and xenophobia through their cultures and surroundings, and they eventually exhibit these ideas in their behavior. The mass influence of family, friends, schools, the media, and other institutions socialize the population by communicating what behavior is typically good or bad. These influences teach us as a society what to expect of our friends, our families, and ourselves. Children learn the ways to belong to their correct cultural label, whatever it may be. They acquire a sense of their own self-worth, as well as the worth of the social group to whom they relate. Although children develop into freethinking adults capable of making personal decisions, the range of conceivable values, beliefs, and assumptions from which they draw when making those decisions is defined by the societies in which they were raised and those in which they live as adults. The groups with which we identify influence the individual values we hold. Although personal experiences are the primary impact, we define ourselves via the cultural lens through which other members of our society and other societies see us. Thus, although culture is formed on a very individual level, it is maintained and exists within a much larger societal and organizational context. This overarching influence on individuals leads us to conclude that culture is not something that we can easily change or make conscious choices about; it is a part of who we are, and it is irrational.

Cultural Nuances

Clashes between various cultures occur in part because of the variety of different values and behavioral norms to which different cultures adhere, and also because many groups and individuals desire recognition of their own ideologies as the best or most correct. Listed below are a series of cultural nuances. While reading through them, try to decide which ones you would be comfortable with and which ones would cause you discomfort. Which ones do you believe are rational? As a leader, consider if you have employees with some of the following beliefs and behaviors and try to figure out the many ways they could be perceived.

- Using the left hand in some Asian, Middle Eastern, and African cultures is considered inappropriate because it is seen as unclean.
- Wearing leather is offensive in India because cattle are sacred.
- In some Chinese cultures, wearing a green hat is symbolic of an unfaithful wife.
- In Iceland the telephone directory is alphabetized according to first name because last names in Iceland are not passed down in families, but are patronymic, meaning they are derived from the father or mother's first name (e.g., Jonsson or Jonsdottir for the son or daughter of Jon).
- In Brazil, terms like "negao," which refers to a Black man, or "bronco," which refers to a White person, can be considered derogatory or friendly depending on the tone of the speaker.
- Women in Saudi Arabia are forbidden to drive a car.
- In southern China, tapping two fingers on the table is seen as a sign of gratefulness.

- In Fiji, crossing one's arms is seen as a sign of respect.
- Having a conversation with your hands in your pockets makes a poor impression in Belgium, France, Finland, Sweden, and Indonesia.
- Patting someone on the head is a grave offense in Thailand and Singapore because the head is sacred.
- Making eye contact is offensive in Korea, Japan, China, and some other Asian countries.
- In Germany and Poland, switching from a last-name to first-name basis in a relationship is such an eventful passage that it is often marked by clasping arms and downing a ceremonial drink.
- Arranged marriages are a very common tradition in China, India, the Middle East, and Africa.
- In Bulgaria, the head motion for "yes" and "no" are exactly the opposite as in much of the Western world.
- Those who practice it see the African ritual of cutting off a girl's genitals as rational; however, for much of the world, it is seen as barbaric, uncivilized, and sexist.
- In many countries, bribing is the common way to conduct business, but in other countries it may land someone in jail.

This list is only a very small portion of the unique cultural norms and values one can run into when interacting with people from cultures other than one's own. Considering these tremendous variations in cultural norms, it is clear that the differences we see have very little to do with biology and almost everything to do with the values each society places on behaviors. These varied values are at the root of the tremendous conflicts between different cultural groups and within each cultural group. We often have very little knowledge about how other value systems work and adhere to the steadfast belief that one particular behavior or belief—usually our own—is superior to all others. Clearly, this dynamic can affect business and cause irreparable harm if companies cannot find a way to uphold their own values and maintain business relationships with other cultures.

For example, consider the experience of one female executive from a large financial company in the United States who was supposed to go to Japan to do business with a Japanese company. The Japanese company contacted the American financial institution to request a male employee, but was sternly told that if they could not work with the woman, they could find another company with which to do business. The chairman of the American company decided to attend the initial meeting, and by showing his support for the female employee and his respect for the Japanese business, an agreeable solution was found. The female employee led all of the meetings over the course of the visit and the Japanese company decided she was an acceptable business partner. This cultural problem was handled in a respectful, empathetic manner, which led to a more productive relationship for the two companies and an improved situation for the female executive.

Like the chairman of the American company, leaders must truly exhibit the values of inclusivity by proactively and visibly supporting diverse individuals in leadership positions and throughout the organization.

Our Diverse World

It would be nearly impossible to calculate how many different societies, cultures, and ethnic groups make up our world's population of seven billion. An ethnic group is defined as a collection of human beings who identify with each other based on a real or presumed common heritage. Ethnic identity is further marked by recognition by others that a group shares distinct and common cultural, linguistic, religious, behavioral, or biological traits. This distinctiveness can also be either real or presumed.

Before going into more detail concerning the complexities of our cultures, briefly consider these facts:

- In 2009, Africa represented 14.4 percent of the world's population. In 2050, that number will rise to 20.2 percent.
- Asia currently represents 60.7 percent of the world's population; in 2050, it will have dropped to 58.5 percent.
- Latin America and the Caribbean represent 8.7 percent of the world's population. In 2050, that figure will only have dropped 1/10 of a percent.
- Oceania, comprised of Australia, New Zealand, and the other islands of Melanesia, Micronesia, and Polynesia, currently represents 0.5 percent of the world's population and in 2050 that will still be true.
- Currently, Europe represents 10.5 percent of the world's population; in 2050 that number will drop to 7.3 percent.

- Despite the economic and militaristic domination of the world by the United States, only about 5 percent of the world's population lives in North America. In the year 2050, approximately the same percentage will still reside in North America.

As these numbers indicate, over the next forty years the world population by continent will remain quite stable except on two continents: the African percentage of the world's population will increase by 5 percent and the European percentage will decrease by about 3 percent.

In other words our world, which is primarily made up of people with various shades of brown skin, is becoming more Brown and less White. With our increasingly globalized world and increased immigration, this trend will be seen throughout the world. In some White populations, this "browning" of the world is seen as a huge threat to their existence, wellbeing, and cultural values.

While it is a common fallacy to equate culture with ethnicity, these two concepts of identity do not always coincide. Consider the following example to help contextualize how important these differences are. Juan Garcia and Rodrigo Alvarez are both of mixed American Indian and European heritages. Although their ethnic makeup is the same, Juan lives in urban Los Angeles, California, does not speak Spanish, and aligns his values with typical American ideals. Rodrigo, on the other hand, lives and works on a ranch in rural Mexico, speaks Spanish exclusively, and is very proud of the indigenous traditions passed down from his parents. While these men share common ancestry, their cultures are clearly made up of many other factors.

As seen in many parts of the world, the more that people of different ethnicities interact with each other, the more homogenous culture becomes. Countering this homogenization is a dramatic resurgence of tribalism, religious fascism, xenophobia, ethnocentrism, and uncompromising political fascism. While many smaller indigenous societies are disappearing into national societies, some larger ethnic groups are violently reasserting their independence from the nations of which they have been a part.

One example of this is Yugoslavia being broken up into ethnically "pure" areas during the 1990s, or the very prevalent "tribal" reemergence that has occurred throughout Eastern Europe and all over the former Soviet Union. The reemergence of ethnic and class strife also appears in China, India, various parts of South America, and the Middle East. Unfortunately, what spawns from this tribalism are ruthless genocidal conflicts, as evidenced in parts of Africa, especially the Sudan, Somalia, Rwanda, and the Democratic Republic of Congo. But let us not forget that many of the boundaries and nations in conflict were not created by the people that live in them but by former Western colonial powers.

Of course, it is also important to remember that clashes often occur within ethnic groups, as in Northern Ireland, and across ethnic divides, such as the severe split between fundamental conservatives and radical progressives in the United States. These divides occur in part because of the various ways we construct our cultural identities. There are many aspects that create our cultural identity, but there are three important facets that are most important to consider: ethnicity, language, and religion.

Ethnic Identity

Ethnic identity can be described as the awareness of belonging to an ethnic group, with all the values and feelings that this membership evokes. It is important to realize that this identification is not necessarily synonymous with one's cultural or racial identity. The word ethnicity is more exclusive than the word race because it carries a finer distinction—although people might be of the same racial classification they can each have very different ethnic backgrounds.

One such example of this is comparing Northern Europeans in places like Ireland or Finland to European Hispanics from Spain. Although both groups have white skin and consider themselves European, each one has distinctive ethnicities and different cultures. Similarly, this type of categorization occurs among the many African countries. In Nigeria, the most populous country in Africa, people say they are Nigerian but classify themselves as Igbo (Ibo), Yoruba, or one of the many other ethnic groups.

Another example of the complexity in distinguishing between culture, race, and ethnicity can be seen in the spread of Hispanic culture around the world. As Central and South America were colonized by Spain, Hispanic ideals were imposed upon the indigenous peoples of the region, along with the Africans who were brought to the area by Spanish slave owners. Later on, immigrants who came to the "new world" from areas like Italy, Germany,

Japan, China, or Portugal also adopted this Hispanic culture. Although this mass group of people shares similar customs, languages, and religions, they identify with a variety of different racial and ethnic backgrounds.

To highlight the complexities of nationality and ethnicity, consider the following countries' ethnic makeup:

Australia	92% White, 7% Asian, 1% Aboriginal and other
Brazil	53.7% White, 38.5% mixed White and Black, 6.2% Black, 0.9% other (includes Japanese, Arab, Amerindian), 0.7% unspecified
Canada	28% British Isles origin, 23% French origin, 15% other European, 2% Amerindian, 6% other (mostly Asian, African, Arab), 26% mixed background
China	91.5% Han, 8% ethnic minorities (55 reported including Zhuang, Manchu, Hui, Miao, Uyghur, Tujia, Yi, Mongol, Tibetan, and Buyi)
Germany	91.5% German, 2.4% Turkish, 6.1% other (made up largely of Greek, Italian, Polish, Russian, Serbo-Croatian, Spanish)
India	72% Indo-Aryan, 25% Dravidian, 3% Mongoloid and other
Iran	51% Persian, 24% Azeri, 8% Gilaki and Mazandarani, 7% Kurd, 3% Arab, 2% Lur, 2% Turkmen, 1% other
Nigeria	Nigeria, Africa's most populous country, is composed of more than 250 ethnic groups; the following are the most populous and politically influential: 29% Hausa and Fulani, 21% Yoruba, 18% Igbo (Ibo), 10% Ijaw, 4% Kanuri, 3.5% Ibibio, 2.5% Tiv
Russia	79.8% Russian, 3.8% Tatar, 2% Ukrainian, 1.2% Bashkir, 1.1% Chuvash, 12.1% other or unspecified

(continued on next page)

(continued from previous page)

United States	72% White, 13% Black, 5% Asian, 0.9% Amerindian and Alaska native, 0.2% native Hawaiian and other Pacific Islander, 3% two or more races
	Note: A separate listing for Hispanic is not included because the U.S. Census Bureau considers Hispanic to mean persons of Spanish/Hispanic/Latino origin including those of Mexican, Cuban, Puerto Rican, Dominican Republic, Spanish, and Central or South American origin living in the U.S. who may be of any race or ethnic group (White, Black, Asian, etc.); about 15.1% of the total U.S. population is Hispanic.

It is important to remember that the degree to which an individual relates to his or her own race, ethnicity, gender, culture, or class can vary greatly. This complex idea often comes into play in a person's social life and personal interactions, but we find that this dynamic also appears within the corporate world. In one seminar ARMC Global conducted on cultural differences and diversity, we observed some interesting behavior regarding identity, ethnicity, and values. An East Indian Asian man who was born into an upper-middle-class Catholic family, spoke fluent Portuguese, and graduated from Harvard University found the most in common with a fellow Harvard graduate who was also raised Catholic and spoke Portuguese. Although the other man was of lower-class Cape Verdean, African, and Portuguese descent, the similarities in language, religion, and education helped them build a common bond.

Another seminar we conducted showed similar results when we paired a young Black woman with a master's degree in public health with a middle-aged White male physician. Despite the obvious difference in their physical appearances, the two found they had plenty in common; both were born in small Indiana towns with well-educated, professional parents working outside the home. One was

Presbyterian while the other was Episcopalian, and both were graduates of Indiana University. This led them to share very similar values about family, education, politics, and government.

Similarly, ARMC Global worked with a Japanese man who was raised in rural Japan by very traditional parents who held both Shinto and Buddhist ideals. The man attended Cambridge University for his undergraduate and graduate degrees, but returned home several times each year. After completing his education, the man saw himself as multi-cultural and comfortable in both Japanese and English environments. He told us that when he was with colleagues, they would comment on how British he seemed, but if they were to come to Japan with him, they would see how Japanese he really was. These additional factors had a much greater impact on the character of his relationships than his race, gender, or age.

All of the above examples prove how our cultural identities are defined by many distinct and different influences. Most of us are the product of multiple heritages and feel ourselves drawn to particular ones at different times in life. Every individual culture is a complex network of combined past experiences and influences that significantly impact the way we behave and perceive the behaviors of others. These varying cultural influences develop our personal values and can help build character that allows us to support one another inside society and organizations. However, if humans fall into biased and closed-minded thoughts and behaviors, tremendous conflict and inefficiencies can and will occur with increasing regularity as people from diverse backgrounds come into contact with each other.

Language

The second important facet of cultural identity is language. Language encompasses not only the spoken word but also the multiple ways we communicate, such as tone, hand gestures, eye contact, or use of personal space. Language makes culture possible because our values and beliefs rest within its framework. It creates the multiple abstractions that govern people's behavior, beliefs, values, and attitudes. Linguists estimate that there are roughly 6,900 languages in the world, the majority of which are spoken by only a small number of people. Some countries are incredibly linguistically diverse, like Papua New Guinea with 820 living languages, or Nigeria with 516 languages. In some countries, this diversity can be problematic, as in India, which has 427 languages, none of which are spoken by a majority of the population. Of course in some countries, such as Iceland, nearly all inhabitants speak one language.

Language is especially important in the business world, as it makes industry possible within and across cultures. As corporations become more global through expansions, acquisitions, and mergers, language often becomes the bridge that unites two unique cultures. When these transitions occur, the corporation establishes operations on the foreign soil of the newly acquired company where the acceptance of different cultures and languages becomes critical to corporate success. Companies must not only learn the language of the new country so that they may deal with the rules, regulations, and government policies of their new setting. They also must hire local employees, necessitating the development of a common understanding of what particular abstract concepts mean in other languages and cultures.

Despite these necessities, language difficulties contribute to conflict and inefficiency in the increasingly diverse organizations around the world. Language is an extremely important part of culture and it shapes behaviors, values, and attitudes. Over ARMCG's years of work, we have conducted seminars with thousands of employees from diverse backgrounds and cultures, and the most frequent problems are those that stem from the areas of language and culture.

Conflicts arise because meaning is often lost in translation. In some instances, concepts and ideas do not have literal translations from one language to another, rendering these ideas nearly useless in business transactions and other corporate situations. For example, some Native American tribes do not have a word that expresses time in the broadly accepted sense. As such, this culture has a different concept of what "time" means and may have different values related to time from most of the other cultural groups of North America. Of course this means that interactions and relationships are potentially difficult unless this is understood.

ARMC Global is confident that mutual discussions based on Trust, Respect, Empathy, and Ethics (Global-TREE^{SM}) will help define the numerous different perspectives. If language shapes the way in which we understand the world, it follows that language should have an impact on shaping our personal values about the world. Several studies demonstrate the validity of this hypothesis. In one such experiment by anthropologist and linguist Peter Farb, bilingual Japanese women were asked the same series of questions, once in English and once in Japanese. The results clearly demonstrate that one's language of expression has a direct impact on the content of the message. Here, for example, is the way the same woman completed the same sentences at the two interviews:

> *"When my wishes conflict with my family's…*
> *…it is a time of great unhappiness."*
> *(Translated from Japanese)*
> *…I do what I want." (English)*
> *"Real friends should…*
> *…help each other." (Translated from Japanese)*
> *…be very frank." (English)*

It is evident that the woman's values relative to family and friends were informed in part by the language that she uses to discuss these concepts. Another study conducted by Ralston, Cunniff, and Gustafson compared responses of bilingual Chinese managers in Hong Kong to a questionnaire about management practices. The managers were asked to respond once in English and once in Chinese. Again, the language in which they responded had an effect on their responses. When responding in Chinese, the managers' answers reflected values related to group harmony and cooperation. But when the same managers responded in English, they expressed values related to individual achievement and competition. As we can see in these examples, leaders who take time to understand how cultural nuances and values are shaped by language will have greater knowledge of how to interact with multicultural groups of employees and an increasingly diverse customer base.

One of the major hurdles in overcoming language

barriers is that many countries are still concerned with protecting their official languages. France is an example of a society making strong attempts to guard its language; in 1994 they induced a law that makes French mandatory on advertisement labels, instruction manuals, and all other consumer documents. About 40 percent of the songs played on French radio must be in French, and a similar requirement exists for television programming. Japan is quite similar. It is very clear to all who live or visit there that Japanese is the only official language of the country. This creates many problems for international businesses interested in interacting with local companies because of the difficulties in learning the language. Compounding this is the fact that even in Japanese companies based outside of Japan, employees frequently speak their own language despite their knowledge of the host country's language. Cultural singularity is a country's continued use of traditional languages and dialects, and people who are unable to communicate because of strong language differences often maintain strong cultural differences as well.

Much of the world's ethnocentrism—and resulting conflict—centers on language. One classic example of a dispute over language is the clash that went on for years between the Germans, French, and English over German becoming the third official language of the European Union. Similarly, in the United Kingdom intense language disputes exist among the various groups of Scottish, Welsh, English, and Irish citizens. The type of ethnocentrism that marks these conflicts is seen throughout the world and is unwise, especially in view of the emerging global marketplace. With the development of instantaneous worldwide communication and rapid transportation that allows business deals to happen globally, one can no longer only be comfortable speaking one's own language, but must also become familiar with other languages and cultures in order to maintain a competitive edge. The EU recognizes how important this is and has developed numerous programs to help make employees multilingual. Corporations absolutely need to adopt this strategy.

Finally, language has a large influence on a culture's marketplace. For example, many large companies have veered dangerously close to international embarrassment when it comes to naming their products. One pharmaceutical corporation wanted to name their weight loss pill "Tegro," which sounds harmless in English, but in French the word is phonetically identical to "T'es gros," which means, "You're fat." Additionally, consider the Parker Pen Company, which marketed the Quink pen with the phrase "It won't leak and embarrass you." In Spanish this campaign translated to the pen that won't "embarazar" you, which literally means that the pen won't make you pregnant. Obviously, these are not quite the messages these companies were trying to convey. When working internationally, companies must constantly stay aware of the market they are trying to reach.

It is very clear that a corporation or organization cannot succeed if it does not understand the various characteristics of the regions in which it hopes to become involved. Furthermore, no company can be competitive in a global marketplace if it remains intolerant of people who speak a language different from their own. If a society or organization wishes to be involved in the evolution of our diverse and interconnected world, it is imperative that each member learn and be conscious of additional languages in order to understand, appreciate, and value different cultures.

Religion

The final factor that contributes to people's cultural identity is religion. Historically, religion and its various beliefs have been embedded into our cultures. Religious ideas differ from ethnicity and language because they deal with our consciousness and our understanding of our own mortality. Religion presents a greater challenge to humans than ethnicity or language because of the intense connection many people feel toward it. Ultimately, when humans face tribulations, they seek a higher belief system to help handle those hardships. Religion allows societies to deal with things that surpass the limits of development or science, despite cultural evolution steadily expanding those boundaries. When considering one's identity, this is a factor that weighs in again and again. Appreciating the significant influence that religion has in most of the world, note the most common belief systems listed below.

Religion in the world

- Christianity: 2.1 billion
- Islam: 1.5 billion
- Secular/Nonreligious/Agnostic/Atheist: 1.1 billion
- Hinduism: 900 million
- Chinese traditional religion: 394 million
- Buddhism: 376 million

- Primal-Indigenous: 300 million
- African Traditional & Diasporic: 100 million
- Sikhism: 23 million
- Juche: 19 million

These religions, and thousands of others in the 20th and 21st centuries, have increasingly come into contact with each other all over the world, in a variety of ways. With the incredible amounts of people following a vast array of differing religions, it is easy to see how conflict can arise. For a better understanding of how religion plays out in various countries, consider the religious makeup of the following countries:

Australia	26% Roman Catholic, 21% Anglican, 21% other Christian, 2% Buddhist, 2% Islam, 1% other, 15% none
Brazil	73.6% Roman Catholic (nominal), 15.4% Protestant, 1.3% Spiritualist, 0.3% Bantu/voodoo, 1.8% other, 0.2% unspecified, 7.4% none
Canada	43% Roman Catholic, 23% Protestant (including 10% United Church, 7% Anglican, 2% Baptist, 2% Lutheran), 4% other Christian, 2% Muslim, 16% none
China	Officially atheist but people practice various religions such as Taoism, Buddhism, Islam, and Christianity
Germany	34% Protestant, 34% Roman Catholic, 4% Islam, 28% Unaffiliated or other
India	81% Hindu, 12% Muslim, 2% Christian, 2% Sikh, and 2.5% of other groups such as Buddhists, Jain, and Parsi
Iran	89% Shi'a Islam, 9% Sunni Islam, 2% other
Nigeria	50% Islam, 40% Christian, 10% indigenous beliefs

Russia	15–20% Russian Orthodox, 10–15% Muslim, 2% other Christian
Spain	73% Catholic, 20% no religion, 10% other religions
United States	52% Protestant, 24% Roman Catholic, 2% Mormon, 1% Jewish, 1% Muslim, 10% none

At the most basic level, religion greatly affects the corporate world. For example, the Mattel office in Malaysia built three different shrines—Hindu, Buddhist, and Islamic—inside its building in order to accommodate its employees' varying religious needs.

Despite the many differing concepts found in the world's religions, we are all still capable of connecting with each other on a basis of understanding, acknowledgment, and tolerance. Unfortunately this type of behavior is not typically the norm.

Religiously motivated violence is a prevailing element of today's conflicts. Consider the rise of Islamic insurgencies throughout many parts of the world. These individuals kill in the name of their God to justify the violent conflicts in which they engage. In the U.S., fundamentalist Christian groups have attacked doctors who perform abortions. Despite those individuals who commit violence in the name of religion, many religions are quite similar at a basic level, particularly Judaism, Christianity, and Islam; each faith promises divine rewards for earthly sacrifice. In each, there is a dark enemy who identifies with evil that a light presence, identified with good, has set out to vanquish. This cosmic struggle between the forces of good and evil leads to monumental philosophical conflicts and often to the unspeakable violence we have seen committed in the name of religion. The historical and ongoing conflicts related to religion affect interpersonal relationships, and this is an extremely important factor for companies to consider. Not only do leaders need to be mindful of particular religious practices and holidays, but also the ideals and beliefs behind these religions and how they might impact business practices, communication, values, interactions, and attitudes. This understanding can only come with more education about and acceptance of all religions that exist.

Conclusion

Culture can be defined as the values, norms, beliefs, and assumptions that translate into the very specific and unique behaviors of variously defined cultural groups. But as we have illustrated, many of those values and norms are subjective and essentially irrational, as they often become ingrained in us at very early ages without our knowledge or choice. The multitude of cultures and sub-cultures interacting with increasing regularity will ultimately lead to opportunities for conflict if each individual does not understand his or her own particular cultural identity while also appreciating and respecting that of others. By finally understanding these things, both parties will be able to determine the impact that implicit and explicit biases, stereotypes, and cultural differences have on interactions, and will identify ways to overcome them.

We all view cultures from within the framework of our own values, norms, and beliefs. Therefore, it is important to constantly remind ourselves that different is neither good nor bad, but simply different. All of this is crucial to building essential skills for managing human resources in a global or multi-cultural context. This more complete understanding will enhance the ability to foster productive relationships with coworkers, customers, and stakeholders. It will assist employees in building Trust, Respect, Empathy, and Ethics (GlobalTREE[SM]) within their relationships and environment, enabling them to become members of truly high performing world-class teams.

CHAPTER 6

Bureaucracies and Hierarchies— Two Necessary Evils

"The disease which inflicts bureaucracy and what they usually die from is routine."

– John Stuart Mill

The History and Evolution of Bureaucracies

Just like human society, bureaucracy has a long history with origins that date back to the domestication of plants and animals thousands of years ago. As domestication progressed, most humans became more sedentary. With the ability to produce surplus food, humans were able to sustain increasingly larger populations. As families began to more easily meet their survival needs, there was more time for activities other than gathering food and creating shelter. At the same time, specific divisions of labor began to emerge.

Prior to the development of agriculture, people in small hunter and gatherer groups had tight and stable cultural rules for interacting with one another. Each person had an intimate relationship with the environment and learned to synchronize with its patterns of change. In these societies, each individual knew every other member of the group and clearly understood their particular relationship. Given that familiarity, codifying the behavioral expectations was unnecessary because the community followed in lock step. If you did not want to behave appropriately you were left to survive on your own, which was not a pleasant option in that environment.

The growth of agriculture-based villages brought together people who had no prior relationships and more complex social structures emerged. These societies are characterized by craft or feudal systems and were lacking in justice, rules, order, and fairness. Nepotism was rampant. Rewards, titles, and promotions were given almost exclusively to prominent and connected citizens regardless of their skill or achievements and the rest of society was left to toil in frustration and accept their lower positions. The unjust nature of these societies made it very difficult to bring together diverse people in a peaceful manner.

To run and manage these societies, hierarchical social systems emerged using increased stratification, specialization, and divisions of labor. A crucial factor for maintaining the peace became the fair and equitable distribution of surpluses, regulated by the rules and laws put forth by the society. To create organizations that could honestly and objectively allocate resources, rewards, and recognition in order to create productive societies with loyal citizens, the structural component of bureaucracies was established. The theoretical design of this model arranged jobs based on organizational needs and featured quick, effective, and consistent decision-making through a chain of command. These strategies allowed for the more efficient practice of the rules and regulations, and created the most competent institutions. The early foundations of Western-style bureaucracy have been built upon, extended, and have evolved into the modern bureaucratic structures we see in all areas of business, government, and society today.

One particularly clear example of the modern evolution of bureaucracy is the explosive success of business in the United States in the late 1800s, despite the inefficiencies that were part of the structure of society prior to the Civil War. This success was based in large part on the institutions of slavery and indentured servitude, but the use of newly constructed bureaucratic structures also played a significant role. The technology of mass production had yet to develop and trade was still local, or at most regional, but the Civil War changed all that. In order to meet the wartime demand for military goods, many businesses had to increase production levels and quickly churn out standardized products, employing specifically skilled workers to get the job done. New technologies that were developed in the industrial revolution made this possible, but many times the older business structure stood in the way. As a result, modern bureaucracies existed in very limited numbers at that time. But only fifty-five years later, during the 1920s, the modern bureaucratic model was very influential and seen throughout the majority of U.S. businesses and in countries like Japan and Germany. In the U.S., bureaucracies became highly developed machines that dominated the industrialized world.

The Western concept of bureaucracy has two primary elements that have significantly altered the way work is conducted: hierarchical structure and scientific management. Bureaucracy replaced the old feudal business structure so completely because it addressed people and technology, the two predominant organizational elements.

In these early feudalistic bureaucracies workers often felt that advancement only came from nepotism and favoritism. Considering that the majority of workers had absolutely no connections, these beliefs greatly lowered morale. When the new bureaucratic structure emerged, it offered real hope to these workers. Each employee was promised a clear career path, as long as he or she performed adequately and did what the bureaucracy asked in written policies and job descriptions. After working and living for so long under the shadow of favoritism and nepotism, the promise of a more merit-based organization was very enticing. During its evolution, bureaucracy changed organizational communication patterns, reporting relationships, reward systems, performance development, job structures, and socialization patterns. It stabilized organizational performance levels and ensured greater equality for more employees. We should note that this discussion of bureaucracy is primarily related to bureaucracies in the Western world. Eastern countries such as China, India, and Japan have their own bureaucratic structures with unique characteristics based on their cultural evolution.

Technology was crucial in the shift from older bureaucratic models to modern bureaucracy because of the incredible advances made between 1860 and 1950. The standardization and constant advancement of tool and machinery products transformed millions of craftsmen into machine-based laborers. What resulted from this development was the emergence of the assembly line, which breaks work into a series of linear tasks, with each set of hands contributing a specialized skill. The success of a bureaucracy depends upon the compartmentalization of tasks to ensure that each set of hands has adequate knowledge. The original feudal structure could not arrange work in this way because it was contingent upon the fabrication of products made by skilled craftsmen. As admirable as that craftsmanship is, the assembly line model, which was better able to meet the increasing demands of the population, displaced it.

By the time modern bureaucracies had largely replaced older forms of bureaucracy, the United States had poised itself to become a fully industrialized nation. Bureaucracy had taught workers the three basic tenets for success in this newly industrialized society: follow the rules; put in your time; get promoted. It also acted as a guideline to the specific structures needed to capitalize on this new mantra. These changes ushered in an age of urbanization, mandatory education, new technologies, and communications media. Most notably for the United States, it was the bureaucracy that transformed the country from an agricultural society into an industrialized one, and many other countries followed suit.

During the 1970s and 1980s, the 1950s model of bureaucracy began to significantly change. Technology had advanced into a world of microchips and computers, blurring and changing the old bureaucratic structure that had been based on command and control. Workforces were becoming more educated and their goals and interests shifted. Employees also began demanding that bureaucracies take note of their desire to be considered individuals rather than cogs in a machine. Yet as bureaucracies progressed into the 1990s and 2000s, many became self-centered and self-sustaining, with little regard for their society or the masses of employees working in them. Today many bureaucracies are run by leaders much more interested in their own wealth and aggrandizement than bringing value to customers, employees, stakeholders, and societies. In too many companies, increasing wealth involves creating paper financial products like derivatives that have questionable assets to back them up, a system that few people understand and from which even fewer benefit.

The "Ideal" Bureaucracy

The greatest promise, and perhaps the greatest failure, of bureaucracy was the idea that it was based on the concept of meritocracy. This system, which seeks to build organizations based on merit alone, also deals with the concept of differentiating the person from the job. Work in bureaucracies is generally defined by the needs of the organization rather than the needs of the people performing the work. Therefore, jobs must be clearly defined in terms of duties, responsibilities, methods, and authority. The chain of command is created by the authority that each position has over the one below it. We refer to this as the model of positional power because the authority lies in the office rather than in the ability of the person who holds the office at a given time. The ideal of positional power is quite different from the practice of positional power in most workplaces. For example, a woman promoted to an executive position in a corporation will maintain a level of power over those in lower positions, simply because she is higher up in the chain of command. However, the ideology of positional power often does not stand up in reality, where numerous factors other than job title affect level of authority. It is possible that even if an extremely qualified woman is promoted, she may not receive the degree of authority entitled to her position simply because there are employees at all levels of the chain of command who have sexist attitudes. It is clear that for the ideals of meritocracy to be realized, companies must build environments based on GlobalTREE^{SM}.

To help envision the bureaucratic structure, a physical pyramid is often used. At the top are a few select individuals whose primary job is to act as a repository for information pertinent to the organization. Supposedly, this top position is awarded because of experience and ability, enabling effective assimilation and distribution of information traveling up the pyramid. These top positions also control and allocate rewards, which of course leads to power and influence. Moving down the pyramid, the number of employees increases, but the amount of strategic information, power, and influence decreases. The very bottom of the pyramid contains frontline workers with the least amount of organizational information and fewest available rewards. Yet it is these workers who work most with clients, generate products, and perform the services that are crucial to keeping the organization afloat and successful. The chain of command helps direct well-marked career paths. Upward movement ensures more power, authority, ability to make decisions, access to information, and, of course, monetary gain and many other perks. The hierarchical structure makes the top position the most desirable career goal for employees, but having that as the sole focus for employees creates many problems.

In theory, banishing all personal relationships and human frailties from the workplace makes it possible for this type of system to function at peak efficiency. Noted sociologist Max Weber believed that effective bureaucracies leveled interest and caused the development of unemotional interactions. Weber posed what he deemed the three most important social consequences bureaucratic systems create:

1. *The tendency to "leveling" in the interest of the broadest possible basis...*
2. *The dominance of a spirit of formalistic impersonality...without hatred or passion, and hence without affection or enthusiasm.*
3. *The dominant norms are concepts of straightforward duty without regard to personal considerations. Everyone is subject to formal equality of treatment.... This is the spirit in which the ideal official conducts his office.*

In his classification, Weber was partially right; but despite the efforts of rules and codifications, several human tendencies will consistently create subjectivity and unfairness. Generally, most humans fear losing what they have and feel a strong need to protect it. Yet, humans also strongly desire what others possess, often perceiving it as better. Within a bureaucracy, there will never be sufficient resources to satisfy all of these needs, whether real or perceived. The outcome of this at every level, in both bureaucracies and societies, is conflict.

Should We Break Down Bureaucracies?

Despite the conflict and inefficiencies bureaucracies can create, they have worked for our societies for a long time. But our world is changing so rapidly that those inefficiencies and conflicts are escalating. Before going any further, consider the following features that define today's business environment.

- Businesses have become highly global, and therefore highly competitive.
- Mergers and acquisitions between businesses occur almost every day, both domestically and globally.
- The life cycles of most products have greatly shortened.
- Most current corporations are only interested in short-term profits instead of long-term gains, not only for the corporation, but also for society as a whole.
- Advanced technologies allow competitors to duplicate and slightly enhance products to turn out "new and improved" ones in only a matter of months.
- Technology also makes it possible for smaller companies with fewer financial resources and less manpower to successfully compete against larger ones.

- Instantaneous global communication is available at all levels of an organization.
- Many employees are culturally, racially, ethnically, and religiously diverse. They are also better educated and more demanding.
- Units within organizations contain multiple generations with different values because humans are living and working longer.
- Today's workforce has become less loyal to their employers and customers have become less loyal to brands. Today, products are expected to add value to our lives using a very individual set of conditions.
- The disloyalty also stems largely from the increasing view that company leaders are out of touch, greedy, self-centered, and often even incompetent, with only their personal fortunes in mind.
- Today's stakeholders have become more vocal about expressing their needs, goals, and the desire for the organization to respect their wishes.

Given the changes in business and society, it is clear that bureaucracy needs to change. The problem is that for the current bureaucratic model to be successful, it is necessary to remove the human from human being. Regardless of their good intentions, the reality is that with dehumanization at their foundation, bureaucratic organizations will continue to be filled with tremendous challenges and conflict.

Many of those who study bureaucracy argue that the purpose behind its rules, regulations, and hierarchies is to eliminate uncertainty, assure control, and promote efficiency. Author Kathy Ferguson disagrees with this and believes that bureaucracies are political organizations that depersonalize social relationships, mystify communications, and disguise dominance. She argues that claims of "efficiency and effectiveness are at best secondary and frequently irrelevant; they are justifications, rather than explanations, of bureaucracy." Those particular facets of bureaucracies actually promote strict adherence to rules, regulations, and procedures. According to Ferguson, the formalized relationships and promise of promotion are actually strategies to control the employees, making them dependent on higher levels of management. This treatment causes anger, alienation, and both physical and emotional problems. These issues result in less productivity, as well as products and services that are lower in quality, which in turn lead to dissatisfied customers and poor economic health of the corporation.

One of the original goals of bureaucracy was to eliminate favoritism and nepotism from professional human relationships. As time went on, the goal shifted to the elimination of any kind of emotion from these relationships. However, we are starting to realize that to remove emotion is to put machine-like standardizations in its place. If that is the case, employees will not feel valued and appreciated enough to work their best. As we can tell from history, bureaucracy was crucial in its initial days, but in the current world in which we live, it must change.

Humanizing Bureaucracies

Sociologist Karl Mannheim believed that one fundamentally flawed characteristic of bureaucratic thought was the treatment of problems as administrative rather than political. He argued that behind the supposedly rational rules of bureaucracies were socially fashioned interests of specific groups. Therefore, order in bureaucracies is not based on reason but on socially conflicting and irrational forces that are eventually accepted as the "rational" order. Leaders will do their best to rethink how they understand the role of humans in the bureaucratic structure. Managing in a bureaucracy is not just a matter of balancing budgets, but is primarily about balancing the power struggles between complex and diverse humans.

The first way to improve is to recognize the humanity of those working in bureaucracies. Many anthropologists agree and argue that bureaucracies fail because they are inhumane. Despite what it has become, bureaucracy is most basically an invention of the human mind. As a human invention with humans working within its walls, it actually has the emotional and mental capacity to fight against the very system that created it. Being so intricately tied to humans, bureaucracies are subject to all the complexities and subjectivities of human behavior, a factor that leaders must not ignore.

One very important aspect of human behavior, and in turn bureaucracies, is mental health. Social psychologist Thomas Pettigrew describes positive mental health as the functioning of all of the following six behaviors:

(1) The mentally healthy individual is self-aware, self-accepting and enjoys a stable identity; (2) an individual's degree of development and actualization of his or her potential is also indicative of positive mental health; (3) so, too, is an individual's integration of the many psychic functions; (4) an individual's autonomy, relative independence from social pressures and ability to act independently under internal controls are also important indicators; (5) the adequacy of an individual's perception of reality...; (6) and finally, positive mental health requires the ability to master one's environment at a reasonable level of competency.

Although some among us exercise all of these behaviors at all times, the vast majority of us frequently have a difficult time with one or more of these. Simply put, we all have problems. It is counterproductive to imagine that humans will simply set aside their personal concerns, their desires and needs, or their mental and emotional issues while they are at the workplace. While leaders can encourage a professional environment in which trust, respect, empathy, and ethics are practiced, they must understand that conflict is bound to arise in any situation in which humans are competing for power, rewards, and promotions.

Psychologist R.W. White's writing underscores the problems with ignoring human nature. White writes, "The constant play of impulse beneath and through the rational, conscious, goal-directed activities of everyday life" shows that "beneath the surface of awareness lies a zone of teeming emotion, urge, fantasy, from which spring the effective driving forces, as well as various disrupting agents in our behaviors." This Freudian suggestion convinces us even more of the complexities that exist within the people around us and within ourselves. We learn and understand how to use coping strategies such as sublimation, repression, projection, and denial, all of which can eventually lead to self-defeating behaviors and poor personal interactions.

Bureaucracies do not consider any aspect of psychoanalysis and believe their hierarchies, regulations, and procedures will be able to control human beings. To counteract this unreasonable assumption, leaders have to first realize that bureaucracies are not some giant undefeatable structure, but actually just an instrument built by humanity. As such, they are subject to the shortcomings that human beings have struggled with throughout the course of our evolution: the imperfect functioning of our brains, our stereotypes, and implicit and explicit biases. They are also subject to the "zone of teeming emotion, urge, fantasy" that exists beneath the surface of all humans, even in the workplace. Once this realization is reached, it becomes obvious that many of the challenges corporations face, especially dealing with bureaucracies, have more to do with the nature of human beings than anything else.

How Rules Become Calcified

Sociologist Max Weber strongly believed that formalized rules and procedures would greatly benefit bureaucracies. Unfortunately, in today's modern corporations those formalities that are set in place to ensure predictable, rational, and efficient functioning do not always have the desired results. This happens because those regulations become absolutes and evolve into ends in themselves. Because of this inflexibility, bureaucracies very rarely adapt quickly and efficiently to unique conditions and new situations outside the boundaries of the rule. In today's world, change is nearly constant and extremely rapid. Sociologist Robert Merton notes that this rapidity of change means "the very elements which conduce toward efficiency in general produce inefficiency in specific instances."

As consultants, the ARMC Global team has worked with corporations and leaders who steadfastly adhere to their original processes, even when it affects their ability to make timely and efficient decisions. We believe there are two reasons for this behavior. The first is that many rule makers base the legitimacy of the rule not on its merit but on its status as an idea that must be followed. The second reason comes from the comfort of the familiarity of how things have always been done. Cultural commentator and author Giuseppe Prezzolini provided this important observation about human response to change:

Propositions that run counter to common morality do not create a desire for that discussion or even contradiction but rather an urge to sidestep, ignore or misinterpret. Life, which is full of such blindness to the most clearly expressed ideas, is ruled not by intellect but by desire and pride. Men want to live, not to understand; and they want to live in their own way. If an idea seems to contradict what they want to believe, they refuse to accept it. If they really understand it, they either suppress it or avert their gaze in order not to see it.

Adding on to this behavioral dynamic is the very human need by some leaders to control any process for which they feel responsible, including protecting it from anyone who wants to usurp or alter it. Therefore, the rules, regulations, and procedures can be viewed as a form of job security. A considerable amount of time and effort has been wasted all over the world trying to prevent innovative thinking in order to preserve the status quo.

Ironically, bureaucracies originally helped societies create flexibility by enabling effective surplus distribution and freeing people from excruciating and all-consuming labor. However, as societies expanded, bureaucracies became rigid and more complex. At first, bureaucracies were able to effectively respond to changes in societies because such changes evolved very slowly. But with an increasingly rapid rate of change, bureaucracies have been unable to effectively respond quickly enough. With the introduction of technology and the globalization of the marketplace, this calcification of rules, and thus structures, has become more severe.

Before going any further, we would like to look at the three biggest factors that inhibit progressive change in bureaucracies: the personalities of leaders, the segmented and structured nature of bureaucracies, and the fallacy that increasing training is always a positive action.

As anyone who works in a hierarchical organization knows, change relies heavily on the personalities of those in charge. In most bureaucracies, leaders must first decide if change is needed and then determine how to execute it. Executives, most often males from society's dominant group, traditionally do not have enough important information about their employees or customers. Their judgments are often influenced by subconscious ideas about the world that are based on personal experiences. Generally, similar people who have similar world and organizational views shape these executives' experiences. Therefore, it is extremely difficult for them to understand the entirety of any given situation, blinding them to the benefits of change. Furthermore, the average leader only has a limited time in his or her position, which creates a very narrow range of options.

Additionally, the segmented and structured nature of bureaucracies often promotes inertia. Most employees find comfort in tradition and generally take criticism of it personally; they usually respond poorly to change, and often with good reason. When change does occur, bureaucracy's formalized relationships are replaced with new ones. Restructuring is painful, slow, and disruptive to the entire corporation. When bureaucracies perform poorly, new rules are developed in an attempt to prevent further mistakes or repetition of past mistakes. Over time, these reactionary rules become so cumbersome that an employee's focus shifts to following rules instead of doing the job. The rules transform employee behavior, and the idea of change is only perceived as forced behavioral change—a highly unattractive concept. Thus, a strong inherent resistance to change exists within bureaucracies, especially when the changes are extensive and costly.

Finally, while this idea may be counterintuitive, we find that too much technical knowledge can prevent innovation. Although having technical skills is absolutely essential, if the training to develop those skills is too specific and narrowly focused it can prevent an employee from recognizing different conditions that require new procedures. Too much experience in one area can become limiting and lead to additional inflexibility in the organization.

The Waste of Knowledge-Based Resources

The calcification and inflexibility of bureaucracies eventually leads to the misuse or waste of knowledge, which can cause employees to make decisions based on incomplete information. In the competitive global marketplace, this is particularly perilous because a company's competitors can quickly capitalize on its mistakes. Additionally, customers are growing less brand-loyal, switching products without a second thought. The customer is usually farthest away from the leader and interaction between the two seldom happens. Yet without even realizing it, the customer has the ability to help change the company. Generally, the frontline workers at the bottom of the hierarchy are closest to those customers, but these employees are rarely valued for the information they possess.

Unfortunately, many leaders do not listen to, or in some cases willfully ignore, the recommendations customers pass on to frontline workers. Some leaders implement customer surveys, letting the results of an impersonal questionnaire guide their decisions instead of listening to their employees. So much important customer information gets filtered or lost and leaders are left to merely guess what the values, attitudes, and norms of their customers are, and they often get it wrong. Effective leaders will employ a variety of techniques to understand their customers, pulling information from customers themselves, employees, and market data.

We have seen that when employees are involved in making decisions, improvements are achieved that leaders alone could never produce. Those gains only happen through the innovation that stems from new and fresh collaborations. But in traditional bureaucracies, employees at the lower levels of the organization are not typically allowed to be innovative. There is limited sharing of ideas, information, experience, or knowledge, and employees rarely challenge their superiors' proposals. Offering ideas to improve the company is not considered a crucial part of an employee's job, despite what many companies say. To do so would disrupt the hierarchical order created by the bureaucracy and might very well ruin a career.

Through studies we have completed over the past fifteen years, we have discovered in most employees an enduring mentality of deference to the hierarchy. Participants were asked to rate their companies on the following questions. Their answers were based on a scale of 1 to 10, 1 being "to no extent" and 10 being "to a great extent." The following scores are averages of employee responses from ten companies.

I share pertinent information with other team members, rather than withhold it to promote my own personal or functional agenda. – 8.3

Team members share pertinent information with other team members, rather than withhold it to promote their own personal or functional agendas. – 6.5

In regards to sharing information, employees are clearly less likely to trust their fellow workers to be forthcoming. Although employees gave themselves higher scores on information sharing, it is not a positive work environment when everyone sees himself or herself as doing better than their coworkers.

The mentality in many of these companies has become very self-centered and protective, especially when it comes to sharing essential information. This kind of environment makes it impossible for corporations to make knowledge-able, informed choices, which in turn prevents them from operating at peak effectiveness.

Lack of Innovation

Active innovation, along with the ability to manage and operate effectively in diverse cultures, is extremely important for corporations to prosper in the twenty-first century. Innovation thrives upon new ideas, unique per-spectives, and the joining of diverse minds to process and evaluate information. Innovation can only emerge out of collaboration. Good can come out of any setback when a wide range of people collaborate on a solution in a creative and non-divisive manner. However, if the organization has not created an environment based on Trust, Respect, Empathy, and Ethics (GlobalTREE(SM)), employees will bring forward new and creative ideas infrequently, if ever. Instead, dysfunctional behavior and stale ideas will domi-nate, and eventually the company will probably fail. For example, Digital Equipment was once a technology leader, but because of the complacency and shortsightedness of its leadership it failed to recognize the shifting landscape of their industry.

Here are two more questions from ARMCG's survey, using the same scale as previously outlined, exhibiting how employees felt about offering new ideas.

I exhibit courage by taking a stand on controversial and unpopular issues. – 7.1

Members of the team exhibit courage by taking stands on controversial and unpopular issues. – 5.9

Once again, employees rated themselves much higher than they rated their team members, but even their opinions on their own willingness to take stands is not very high. Innovation requires that businesses view and treat their employees as their most important resource, second only to their customers. It is employees who enable organizations to develop and produce innovative products. In order for employees to develop these products and services, they must have accurate and timely information.

Unfortunately, as the following data from our survey suggests, many employees do not feel that information is shared effectively.

I have sufficient information to make the "right" business decisions. – 6.0

I am kept informed about matters that affect me. – 6.1

Team members are kept informed about matters that affect them. – 6.8

I have timely, accurate information to make the "right" business decisions. – 7.3

Our data from multiple surveys over the course of many years consistently indicate that employees feel their companies value their rules and procedures over the thoughts and ideas of their staff. Innovation cannot happen if employees do not feel informed about their work or encouraged to assert forward-thinking ideas, even if those ideas are unpopular. It is clear that this is a major barrier to building healthy relationships or reaching maximum productivity, and that is what we are seeing in so many of today's corporations.

Politics

In theory, bureaucracies are based on formal, structured, and impartial relationships. Of course, anyone who has ever worked in a bureaucracy knows there are many additional factors at work. Typically, most bureaucracies contain an additional set of informal relationships based on unspoken rules. Most of them are hidden, especially when they directly contradict the formal protocol. Because of this, most bureaucracies are actually intensely political organizations in which Machiavellian attitudes dominate. Machiavelli believed that political action is motivated by one's own ambition, followed by the fear of another's ambition. Whether intentional or not, many employees operate on these terms in competition for influence, power, money, or status.

But some aspects of these informal relationships are good! These unspoken informalities make up much of the interpersonal politics within a bureaucracy and are absolutely necessary. If such politics did not exist, every person would be forced to follow every rule at all times, and very little innovative thinking would emerge. By helping create the informal networks of an organization, the breaking of rules also helps propel the company toward success by fostering innovation and creating new ideas. In many ways, the art of leading in bureaucracies is a matter of understanding how these processes work and allowing the positive informalities to continue in order to support collective goals.

But despite all the benefits politics can bring companies, political dynamics are still extremely difficult to manage and control. They can very easily spiral out of control and create negative environments. The secrecy involved in these types of politics can affect an employee's view of their colleagues and company. The following questions from our survey show how employees feel about their abilities to be effective despite workplace politics.

I consciously transcend silos to achieve greater organizational results. – 7.3

My team members consciously transcend silos to achieve greater organizational results. – 5.9

There are few hidden agendas. – 5.5

Clearly, these numbers suggest that while employees are able to work through the politics in some ways, there is not trust among coworkers. It is very hard to successfully take advantage of informal relationships because they generally develop as the result of chance personal contacts and the outcome is difficult to manage. Also, many of these interactions are based on subjective factors such as social class, gender, or race, as well as implicit and explicit biases and stereotypes. Because of these factors, many of these informal relationships emerge and function best within homogeneous groups. Trust, respect, empathy, and ethics survive much more successfully in these groups because the members share similar norms, values, and behaviors. However, these values are not as easily shared with those outside the group. Also, when disagreement does arise within the group, it is very hard to resolve since the relationships upon which the group is based are unofficial and informal. The result of each misunderstanding or difference is generally a power struggle.

These informal politics also directly negate the objectivity of bureaucracies. Rewards are not given on the basis of objectively defined processes, but because of perceived status within political networks. Politics in today's bureaucracies create a bit of a catch-22 because although they ease some of the employee's frustrations, they also cause a lot of internal strife. A direct result of that internal strife is unhealthy internal competition. Vertical and lateral competition occurs simply because organizations only have a limited number of resources and rewards to distribute. This competition occurs within relationships, as well as outside of them. In the same manner as in large societies, wars can start over one group attempting to enhance its position economically, socially, or politically. Additionally, organizations intentionally create internal competition by assigning competing objectives to various individual business units. Although intended to stimulate higher levels of productivity, this merely shifts the focus to competing against one another rather than against another company, the actual competition. In this environment, healthy relationships, cross-functioning teamwork, and cooperation are all unlikely to develop.

Homogeneity

The homogeneity that still characterizes most bureaucracies, especially at the top, can take either or both of two forms. The first concerns employees, while the second deals with customers. Both are based on the same overly simplistic and invalid assumption that we are all pretty much the same. We will begin by exploring the homogeneous nature of many groups of employees.

Homogeneity in bureaucracies affects employees in multiple ways. The first deals with workplace equity and includes things like benefits, time off, and holidays. Bureaucracy functions in a way that assumes that everyone is the same, and as such, rules and regulations will impact everyone in the same way. Theoretically, this is how to create an equitable work environment. However, this assumption is patently false; we are all different. Humans have an expansive range of wants, ambitions, and needs; simply ignoring those differences undermines equality. This ignorance about human nature creates malcontent, inequity, and rampantly political behavior, and it also forces conformity of thought. In order to advance in this environment, an employee must not only master the company's spoken and unspoken rules, but also adopt the style and behaviors of a prototypical employee. Simply put, employees must assimilate or find another job.

The result of successful assimilation is a group of people who value the same things, have similar worldviews, and even tend to think alike. In these groups, the commonly shared image of a successful employee is based on those who are already in leadership positions. Not only does everyone think alike, but they also tend to look alike in terms of ethnicity, gender, and background. As such, their behaviors and mannerisms are quite similar. In the United States, those in leadership positions are typically White, upper-class males with educations from Ivy League or regional elite schools. These individuals are in charge of hiring applicants for decision-making positions and are likely to choose other White, upper-class males with Ivy League or elite school educations to fill them. This example clearly shows how institutional racism and sexism is created, denying companies access to a significant portion of talent needed to truly succeed in a competitive global marketplace.

The homogeneity of bureaucracies also has a direct effect upon customers. Leaders in bureaucracies view their customers in the same homogeneous way they view their employees. Without pertinent information, these organizations operate as if the needs, wants, and aspirations of their customers resemble those of their leaders. In particular, the current generational-based attitude shift is causing this gap between bureaucracies and customers to grow even bigger. We broke down the process of a company that is losing its customers into five steps:

- Bureaucracies tend to lose touch with their customers.
- Then, they must guess what their customers want and need.
- They develop products and services with minimal appeal for increasingly diverse populations.
- They adopt marketing strategies on the basis of false assumptions and incomplete data.
- The assumption that their customers were homogeneous proves to be a costly one, leading to severe financial hardship and possible bankruptcy.

Given all of the negativity and inefficiency within most of our bureaucracies, it is abundantly clear that we need to develop a different system that works better, most specifically focusing on all of the varied and unique humans who make up our corporations and our societies.

If Not Bureaucracy, What?

Leaders of highly bureaucratic organizations have expressed a readiness to try new methods of conducting business, but little real change is occurring. We believe this is because they are trying to reorganize the structure of the business, but not the people. People are placed into a newly structured organization and essentially end up making it function in the same ways as before. We have to shift focus from a change in structure to a change in people. Once people change, bureaucratic organizations will have sufficient momentum to transform themselves into post-bureaucratic organizations. Key elements of bureaucracy will remain necessary even in the entirely post-bureaucratic organization, but change really can and will come.

The Structure

It is absolutely crucial for leaders to recognize that regardless of the structure of their organization, if there is no attempt to fix the people issues it will fail. People will quickly recreate the previous organization through their norms, values, and behaviors, and the organization will revert to where it was when it started. The post-bureaucratic organization will be small in texture, but not necessarily in actual size. Despite having thousands of employees, the organization will function as a small, entrepreneurial business with employees working together closely. Smaller groups fit our past evolutionary tendency to live in small groups and also our need to find comfort in more intimate relationships.

Here is how an ideal future might look:

- The post-bureaucratic organization will consist of a network of satellite offices that are physically close to customers and linked to each other by one corporate office. That corporate office will act as a coordinator and enabler for the satellite offices and seldom as a power broker. The corporate office will be staffed primarily by the satellite employees who work there in short eighteen-month rotations. This ensures the corporate office will serve as a storehouse of knowledge, which will be systematically recirculated through the satellite offices. This office cannot deviate from the core values of GlobalTREE^{SM}.

- Each satellite office will be in control of its business. The employees will determine appropriate human resource policies, staffing levels, type and depth of product lines, marketing strategies, alliances, etc. This local control helps keep each office in touch with its customer base, enabling it to develop more appropriate products and services.

- Staff at each satellite office will consist of local employees and those with experience at other satellite offices. Employees will experience a moderate amount of turnover, because satellite offices will shuffle staff to accommodate each other's need for specific expertise.

- High-performing and diverse teams will carry out the work at each satellite office. The prime directive of these teams is to deliver world-class products and services to their diverse customers.

- GlobalTREE^{SM} will operate throughout the organization. To become a leader, employees must always epitomize GlobalTREE^{SM}.

- All employees will be given the opportunity to reflect on their life experiences, implicit and explicit biases, and stereotypes in order for them to understand the ways they work and perceive the world.

- Each employee will be valued for his or her unique contribution and ability to build relationships based on GlobalTREE^{SM}, not for his or her short-term financial achievements for the company.

- Communication will be honest, open, and timely. Employees will be able to access relevant information directly, and will therefore be able to give feedback when and where it will be most valuable.

In this new business universe, the chain of command no longer dictates communication patterns, career paths, or organizational success. Advancement becomes a matter of lateral moves, job rotations, and global assignments. Achieving higher management status will no longer be the only sign that one has made it. The freedom to work without oversight, opportunities to work on key projects, and the knowledge that your coworkers trust and respect your work are increasingly valued. Perks of any kind for leaders, like significant, undeserved bonuses, private dining rooms, preferred parking spots, and vacations, should be kept to a minimum. The reward and compensation system will reflect the size and relative flatness of the post-bureaucratic organization. It will also minimize distinctions by level within the organization; rewards will stem from the collective successes of the organization. For example, every employee's compensation package will have a fixed and variable component, with the latter comprising 60–85 percent of annual compensation. There won't be a guaranteed annual raise for simply doing your job; everyone wants and is expected to always do an outstanding job. Increases in the fixed portion of an employee's pay will come through the demonstration of new skills, the acceptance of greater responsibility, and the success of the whole business unit. This post-bureaucratic model creates a proactively inclusive culture based on GlobalTREE^{SM}. In this culture, every employee has a vested interest in the organization's success. This will stem in part from moderately compensating employees with shares of stock, either newly issued or purchased in the open market.

In the post-bureaucratic organization, decision-making is pushed to the lowest possible level, increasing efficiency and customer satisfaction, as well redistributing power and authority. Customer service representatives who are closest to the customer will have greater decision-making authority. Marketing, manufacturing, and customer service departments will share information during all phases of product development, introduction, and service, creating highly developed and sophisticated communication channels and processes. Cross-training and job rotation inside and outside of one's specialty area will be required to help facilitate understanding and communications. These practices will also help create a common organizational language and increase flexibility in the organization. It is always the flexible, broadly skilled workforce with Global-TREE^{SM} ideals that most quickly and effectively makes the changes required to be successful.

Guiding Principles

Exactly how a specific organization adopts and installs the structural components outlined above will vary with the country's labor laws and the business's history, sector, size, workforce makeup, etc. Five specific factors must be in place for the post-bureaucratic model to work:

(A) Diversity has to exist at all points within the organization. The commitment to Proactive Inclusion® should be broad-based and include observable differences in all dimensions of the company.

(B) Innovation and diversity of thought must be seen as an asset. Someone who proposes different, and perhaps difficult, but creative leading-edge ideas must be rewarded, regardless of how he or she is perceived.

(C) Systems and processes that create friction have to be thrown out. Communication patterns need to be based upon everyone's actual knowledge, not on politics or status.

(D) The nurturing of trust, respect, empathy, and ethics in internal and external relationships must be present. Each concept requires open conversations initiated and sustained by leaders who actually live by their core principles.

(E) Fair employment policies and practices need to be

developed to ensure that the organization celebrates differences in the workplace.

These five facets can guide organizations toward increased productivity. But to be truly successful, all post-bureaucratic organizations must commit to working toward the actions listed below.

- Adopt GlobalTREE^{SM} and Proactive Inclusion® as the foundations for the new organizational structure.
- Change and create leadership development and training programs, as we have discussed throughout the book.
- Engage in conversations to develop shared goals, values, and codes of conduct. Leaders must discover what is important to employees, customers, and stakeholders. This will help the organization deliver value and merge the goals of employees, customers, and stakeholders with those of the organization. In this way loyalty is created, solutions are freely offered, obstacles are easily overcome, complaints subside, productivity and performance increase, and the excitement of being a part of the organization becomes infectious.
- Focus on innovation. Organizations gain and maintain their competitive advantage through innovation and the post-bureaucratic structure must consciously strive to foster it. Innovation requires constructive conflict based on

GlobalTREE^{SM}. Different people with different ideas must challenge one another and suggest alternatives to every approach.

- Cultivate and use the entire available knowledge base. In contrast to bureaucracies, post-bureaucratic organizations recognize that only a limited amount of the knowledge needed for success comes from the leader. The leader needs to share organizational strategies with employees, customers, and stakeholder groups, and must also listen to each group's comments and complaints, later incorporating solutions into the strategies. Leaders must consciously bring employees, customers, and stakeholders into decision-making processes by forming diverse high-performance teams.

- Constantly be aware of cultural differences. In the post-bureaucratic organization, team members will be asked to consciously work to understand different ethnicities, religions, genders, sexual orientations, and other differentiating factors. Leaders encourage team members from diverse backgrounds to share their experiences and perspectives. Leaders will acknowledge the barriers that exist and work to eliminate them. Leaders will also discuss diversity regarding customers and demand that all employees provide all customers with fair and equitable service. Finally, all members of the organization will ask themselves how stereotypes impact their own decision-making processes and behavior, while continually trying to minimize the amount of institutional racism and sexism.

All of these concepts can be implemented in work environments when leaders and employees draw upon the incredible knowledge we have within us. Once we have an understanding of what makes our brains react in certain ways and why we view the world in the ways we do, companies can fully prosper and succeed by reaping all the rewards of knowledge and understanding.

Conclusion

We have seen how bureaucracy has helped businesses to succeed throughout the history of humans. Yet today's changing global economic circumstances have exposed numerous flaws in the structure and made clear the need for a new version of management. Bureaucracies make power-based decisions, whereas post-bureaucratic organizations make influence-based decisions. Relationships and communications in bureaucracies are constrained largely by status considerations, and in post-bureaucratic organizations these are free because they are based upon GlobalTREE^{SM}. Bureaucracies function as secretive and obsessively closed-off units while post-bureaucratic organizations are open enough to truly value feedback from employees, customers, and stakeholders. Success in a bureaucratic organization comes from knowing the rules and regulations and how to navigate the politics, but one succeeds in a post-bureaucratic organization by utilizing all knowledge and skills to build beneficial relationships.

Becoming a post-bureaucratic company will have a positive impact on the treatment and job satisfaction of all employees, regardless of their diverse backgrounds. Organizations will need the expertise of all kinds of employees to understand the growing diverse market segments. With the leveling of hierarchies and the diminishing of positional power, employees of this new structure will find that many of the barriers they traditionally face have broken down, enabling them to better contribute to the successes of their organization.

CHAPTER 7

Cultural Clashes Among Diverse Teams

"Insight, I believe, refers to the depth of understanding that comes by setting experiences, yours and mine, familiar and exotic, new and old, side by side, learning by letting them speak to one another."

– Mary Catherine Bateson

As we have outlined in previous chapters, many companies today cannot effectively compete in the increasingly connected global marketplace. The current traditional bureaucratic structure is becoming a source of competitive disadvantage in today's dynamic and constantly evolving global economy. Over the past twenty to thirty years, this disadvantage has worsened, as short-term focus, dysfunction, and greed in many of our modern leaders dominate more beneficial ancestral leadership qualities. While most corporations understand the value of teams and have developed strategies to enhance their effectiveness, companies with high-performing and diverse teams based on

GlobalTREE^{SM} are few and far between. As we will discuss in this chapter, those companies who fail to foster trust, respect, empathy, and ethics will have difficulty building and maintaining productive, successful teams, and will be unable to effectively manage conflict.

How Employees Rate Themselves and Their Teams

In more than thirty years of consulting with organizations around the world, ARMC Global has found that most are not good at creating and maintaining high-quality, effective teams over significant periods of time. To demonstrate our point, we have included data from employees from different business units within ten corporations. We asked them the level to which they agree with the following statements regarding team mission, vision, goals, and objectives, which are crucial factors in building teams.

As with other questions from the study, we used a scale from 1 to 10 with 10 being "To a Great Extent" and 1 being "To No Extent." In the following charts we provide the highest scores, lowest scores, and the average scores from various units in the ten companies.

The significant impact leadership has on team effectiveness is evident in these results and the results of many of our other surveys. Those who act in ways similar to ancestral leaders received higher marks on all of the questions compared to those who exhibited current-day leadership values and behaviors.

Mission, Vision, Goals, and Objectives

Statement	Highest Score	Lowest Score	Average Score
The vision and mission of the team has been defined.	8.4	5.2	6.8
The vision and mission of the team are accepted by everyone.	8.4	5.8	6.4
The objectives and goals of the team have been clearly defined.	8.3	5.9	6.3
The objectives and goals of the team are accepted by everyone.	8.3	5.3	6.8

As the data suggest, some business units are very clear about their vision while others are not. We believe these numbers are greatly impacted by each team leader's ability or inability to effectively engage all team members in the process of defining the vision, and we find these efforts are most successful when GlobalTREE[SM] is present. If there is no definitive set of goals and objectives, team members develop their own, which usually conflict with each other and with the company's stated mission.

A company's norms, values, and behaviors are directly related to the company's mission, vision, and goals. These are published and disseminated widely throughout the organization, but when it comes to implementation, companies often fail miserably. As the following data suggest, significant work is needed to take these statements from the walls to the halls.

Norms, Values, and Behaviors

Statement	Highest Score	Lowest Score	Average Score
The team has developed values, norms, and behaviors that have been entirely understood by all members.	7.8	5.4	6.1
There is a lot of discussion among team members; everyone is encouraged to participate.	8.5	6.1	6.7
When it comes to the important decisions, the goal is to arrive at a substantial—but not necessarily unanimous—agreement, by means of open and thorough discussion of everyone's ideas.	8.5	6.6	7.2

Overall, participants gave lowest marks to the development of values, norms, and behaviors that are understood and accepted by all team members In discussing the results with survey participants, ARMCG has found that companies put great effort in developing appealing concepts on paper but they fall short on efforts to get all employees to truly understand and accept their mission and vision. Without a common understanding, it is difficult to get everyone on the same page, a crucial first step in order to get teams to perform at high levels.

Every organization with which ARMCG has worked has emphasized the importance of such crucial factors as trust, respect, empathy, and ethics. However, in every survey we have conducted these factors generally receive the lowest scores, as the data below indicate.

Trust, Respect, Empathy, and Ethics

Statement	Highest Score	Lowest Score	Average Score
There is a high degree of trust among all team members.	8.4	4.3	6.2
Each team member demonstrates empathy for others.	7.4	4.6	6.0
There is a high degree of respect among all team members.	8.6	4.8	6.0
The work climate fosters ethical risk taking.	7.9	4.7	6.2
As a result of the aforementioned trust and respect, team members have a great deal of confidence in one another.	7.9	4.2	6.3

The lowest scores and average scores show how much work needs to be done to build trust, respect, empathy and ethics in many organizations. The lack of a healthy and productive environment based on GlobalTREE[SM] greatly impacts all aspects of a company's missions, values, team effectiveness, and ultimately the overall functioning of the organization.

The Barriers to Creating Effective Teams

In the previous chapters, we noted a number of factors that get in the way of employees functioning effectively as individuals and in teams. The most important of these factors is the employees' desire for their leaders to exhibit ancestral leadership traits, which is an expectation that is rarely met.

Next in importance is simply the nature of human beings and our various shortcomings: the misfiring of our brains, our tendency to stereotype, and the common belief that our norms, values, and behaviors are better than others', which in turn makes us believe we are more deserving of rewards than others.

Also, most bureaucracies are not structured to support the overall wellbeing of the group, and are instead working to foster competition among employees. All of these factors contribute to the challenges of forming effective teams. The result of these shortcomings is that when diverse people and perspectives come in contact with one another, they often clash.

In addition to these patterns and behaviors, there are a few more trends in business that pose challenges to forming and being part of diverse, high-performing teams.

- Change occurs more frequently than ever before. In many societies, change is lightning fast. We see it in economies, globalization efforts, governments, societal norms, demographics, technologies, and relationships.
- Today's products and services are becoming more complex.

- To create sophisticated services and products and solve the complex problems associated with them, business teams are becoming more complex.
- Teams must become increasingly multifunctional, multidisciplinary, and cross-organizational.
- As products become more and more complex, like the Dreamliner passenger planes or the F-35 fighter jets, their parts come from more companies and countries. To successfully manufacture these products, employees need to be able to communicate with the other companies involved in the process.
- Teams are growing in size to address the increasing complexities of products and services. This drastic increase in size means that there are more relationships that must be managed and maintained, with larger numbers of people with very different languages, cultures, and values.
- The customer base is becoming more global and diverse; customer tastes and needs are becoming very fluid, sophisticated, and demanding. More diverse, creative, knowledgeable, and flexible teams are necessary to better understand this changing customer base.
- The constant downsizing, rightsizing, layoffs, takeovers, and buyouts have resulted in decreased employee job security and have

created a great deal of distrust and lack of loyalty among employees.

- While employees are consciously aware that
they must put aside their egos and work for
the common good, the need to do so conflicts
subconsciously with their desire to compete as
individuals.

- Today's diverse workforce is more educated, has
greater access to information, and is more connected to each other and the rest of the world
through social networks and new technologies.
This modern workforce is making increasing
demands on leaders, many who are ill prepared
to meet these new demands, either because
they do not understand these shifts or they do
not care to spend resources to truly confront
change.

A Recipe for Cross-functional, High-performing, and Diverse Teams

The following are some essential ingredients necessary
for cross-functional, high- performing, and diverse global
teams. Without these traits and characteristics, malaise,
dysfunction, and human shortcomings can take over and
lead to significant conflicts and issues.

- Teams are made up of a small number of
diverse, interdependent, and very self-aware
people.

- The glue that holds each team together is GlobalTREE^{SM}.
- The environment is characterized by truly open and honest communications among the parties involved.
- Lying, sugarcoating the truth, misleading, avoidance, etc. are absolutely not tolerated.
- Honesty is sacrosanct.
- Team members constantly interact with a diverse group of people inside and outside of their organization.
- Team members use a variety of methods to evaluate themselves and the team.
- Team members have complementary skills and are personally committed to a common mission, vision, and purpose.
- Team members share performance goals for which they hold themselves and their team members accountable.
- Team awards outweigh individual awards.
- Power is shared and decisions are made through a collaborative process, but complete agreement is not necessary.
- Conflict is common and openly expressed, yet it is also constructive because it is expected and managed in productive ways based on GlobalTREE^{SM}.
- The focus of the team is both on task behaviors and interpersonal behaviors.
- The top priority of the members is not competition or the needs of the individual, but rather

the integration of their talents, skills, and abilities through collaboration in order to meet organizational, team, and personal goals.

Six Steps toward Building Effective Diverse Teams

Before elaborating on these six steps, it is crucial to note that unless organizations expend considerable effort assisting their employees in understanding themselves and the way they see the world, their teams can never function at the highest levels.

Step One: Self-Assessment

- Each team member will periodically conduct self-assessments to ensure an understanding of strengths, weaknesses, and the origins of personal values and behaviors.

Step Two: Define the Mission

- Have a clear purpose: The vision, mission, goal, or task of the team has been defined and is accepted by everyone.
- Define clear and positive values, norms, and behaviors: The team has developed values, norms, and behaviors that are entirely understood and accepted by all the members, ensuring better communication among them.
- Assign specific responsibilities and expectations: There are clear, fairly distributed

responsibilities and expectations for each team member. Team members accept and carry out their responsibilities with enthusiasm.

- Develop action plans: Action plans are developed that contain specific responsibilities, steps, and deadlines.
- Shared leadership: Although the team has a formal leader, leadership functions shift depending on circumstance, on the needs of the group, and on the skills of the members. The responsibility of the formal leader is to model the appropriate behaviors of our ancestral leaders, which will help establish positive norms more aligned with our human natures.
- Embrace the diversity of styles: The team contains a broad spectrum of player types, including members who stress attention to tasks, goal setting, and the overall process. It contains promoters, analysts, and those who question how the team is functioning. It also includes those members who are introverts or extroverts.

Step Three: Establish and Instill Team Values

- Develop trust: There is a high degree of trust and confidence among all team members.
- Develop respect: As a result of trust and confidence, team members have a great deal of respect for one another. This is the underpinning for teams to act in empathetic and ethical manners in all of their relationships.

- Practice empathy: Team members try to walk in each other's footsteps before judging.
- Act ethically: Team members are committed to acting with fairness, trust, and reliability in all business and personal matters.
- Recognize employee value: Members recognize that each person has strengths and weaknesses, but everyone is valued as long as the job is done well and 100 percent effort is exerted.
- Accept diversity: Team members, customers, stakeholders, and all communities are understood, valued, respected, and appreciated regardless of any dimension of diversity.
- Develop external relations: The team spends time developing key outside relationships, mobilizing resources, and building credibility with important players in other parts of the organization and community.

Step Four: Stipulate the Proper Operational Behaviors

Encourage employees to strive toward the following behavior:

- Listen: Team members use effective listening techniques, such as questioning, paraphrasing, and summarizing to elicit the best responses and fully understand their fellow team members.
- Have open and proactive communication: Team members are free to express their feelings about both the task and group's attempt to fulfill goals.

They recognize and accept the concept of communication in which employees actively seek out information.

- Participate: There is a lot of opportunity for discussion and everyone is encouraged to participate.
- Cooperate: Team members cooperate by generating excitement, achieving goals, and supporting each other. Within groups, members consciously acknowledge the need to be open and forthcoming with their ideas.
- Have productive conflict: Conflicts and disagreements inevitably arise, but the team is comfortable with handling these. They understand the importance of not attempting to avoid, smooth over, or suppress conflicts and disagreements. There are few, if any, hidden agendas.
- Make consensual decisions: When it comes to important decisions, the goal is to arrive at a substantive, but not necessarily unanimous, agreement by means of open and thorough discussion of everyone's ideas.
- Make compromises: Compromises are important, as long as they do not adversely affect the quality of the products or services provided.
- Develop a good climate: The successful and harmonious work climate fosters risk-taking. Failures are seen as opportunities to learn rather than reason to criticize or punish.

Step Five: Continually Compare the Team's Realities with Its Principles of World-Class Products and Services

- Create effective processes: Team members are committed to quality processes and understand the intimate linkage between diversity, Proactive Inclusion®, GlobalTREE℠, and world-class products and services.
- Always improve: Team members are committed to improving processes and creating new and innovative ways to eliminate waste and remedy defects.
- Foster client/customer relationships: Team members are totally committed to meeting customer needs in the most cost-effective and hassle-free manner. They constantly recognize that they are totally interconnected with their customers during both good and bad times.

Step Six: Continually Assess Progress

- Conduct team self-assessment: Periodically, the team examines how well it is functioning and what may be interfering with its effectiveness The team develops proactive, innovative solutions to solve major roadblocks.
- Allocate rewards appropriately: While the individual is still rewarded and recognized, the team as a whole receives the greatest amount of recognition and reward. Team rewards and recognition will reinforce the idea of team cooperation and effort.

The Role of the Leader

In order for companies to meet the challenges of modern business, they must build diverse, world-class, high-functioning teams. In order for these teams to be successful, each member must internalize the principles of trust, respect, empathy, and ethics, and they must also believe that the entire company operates in the same manner. This means that GlobalTREE^{SM} must govern all relationships, activities, and communications in the organization. This can only happen through meaningful action and not simply through a decree from the CEO or through slogans pasted on the walls. The key is for executives to truly live and model these behaviors. However, as daily news accounts suggest, this is not happening in most companies. Instead, we are seeing leaders take action and implement policies that cause employees to believe that neither the organization nor fellow employees can behave ethically, be trusted, or deserve any amount of respect or empathy.

The following are some common organizational patterns and behaviors that we have seen that undermine the values of trust, respect, empathy, and ethics.

1. Leaders not practicing the company's stated values. Many leaders do not adhere to the same rules and values they expect of their employees, touting the old saying, "Do as I say, not as I do."

2. Untimely and inaccurate communication. Leaders must create an environment in which employees feel that their input is valued and used. Organizations undermine

GlobalTREE^{SM} when their leaders do not motivate employees to share information directly and efficiently, or when leaders do not share information themselves. Without this kind of environment, employees rely on the grapevine rather than on official company communications.

3. Downsizing and layoffs. Organizations with a track record of consistently downsizing and implementing layoff programs undermine GlobalTREE^{SM}. These actions shake employee loyalty, hope, and goodwill, while forcing employees to waste time looking for opportunities outside the organization. Employees' energies are spent looking out for themselves rather than for the customer and company. This cycle perpetuates distrust and greed among employees, further spreading the dysfunctional behavior exhibited by their leaders.

4. Special standards for executives. Organizations that give special rewards to executives undermine teamwork and get in the way of productivity. These policies fail to encourage or motivate employees, instead leading them to become dissatisfied and resentful. Senior executives need to be held accountable not only for the success of the company, but for the failures as well. Paying themselves large bonuses while laying off employees is very detrimental to creating GlobalTREE^{SM} and high-performance teams.

5. Lack of or inaccurate performance feedback and career development. Leaders who promise their employees career advancement and endless opportunities are feeding them unrealistic expectations. We have found that many leaders

have a tendency to overlook weaknesses and the need for development and training until after damage is done. In environments like these feedback from employees is often ignored, which leads employees to become angry, hostile, and distrustful of their company and its management.

Managing Conflict

When leaders commit themselves to the values of Global-TREE^{SM}, it permeates the workplace environment; employees are more focused, more dedicated, and more likely to find common ground with their coworkers. However, it is totally unrealistic to think that conflict will not occur. Many corporations are still unable to deal directly, openly, empathetically, and honestly with these conflicts, but blame does not solely fall on their shoulders. From an early age, most of us have been trained to avoid the unpleasantness of conflict and do not want to be seen as someone who rocks the boat. The urge to conform is compounded by the conventional structure of modern bureaucracies. Corporations prefer to avoid conflict because they believe the effect will be devastating, both internally and externally, and because they don't know how to deal with conflict constructively.

One obvious and unpleasant result of conflict is litigation and the resulting judgments against organizations. Other costs are incurred as well, such as negative publicity, lost business, reduced productivity, a decline in the quality of customer service, low morale, wasted energy, and missed opportunities. Yet despite all the pressures to conform, to not rock the boat, and to avoid conflict, each employee is an individual with a unique set of values, ideas, and shortcomings, which can ultimately lead to various types of conflicts. It is important to be prepared for conflict and to understand that, if managed properly, conflict can help the company grow and improve.

Business coach and mediator Dina Lynch has calculated the costs of conflict to organizations. Her conclusions reveal that "managers spend up to 20 percent of their time resolving disputes. For each manager earning $60,000/year, the company is spending $12,000/year on conflict resolution. For managers with higher salaries, the figure can climb to as much as $50,000 or higher/year." We must keep in mind that Lynch's analysis deals only with the conflicts that are made public and does not include those hidden beneath the surface. These hidden internal issues still have similar negative impacts on employees, customers, and stakeholders and significantly impact the bottom line.

Dealing with Conflict Constructively

The problem with conflict is not its existence, but how it is managed. In order to manage effectively, one must have an extensive knowledge of conflict itself. Thus, it is important to acknowledge the two different types of conflict: interpersonal conflict and operations conflict. Interpersonal conflict arises from disputes between people as a result of differences related to personality, style, age, ethnicity, gender, culture, language, and the like. These types of conflict are counterproductive in business situations because they cause employees to become obsessed with personality and character, rather than focusing their efforts on doing the best job possible. By contrast, operations conflict has nothing to do with personal issues. It grows from debates inside corporations. This type of conflict can be positive because rather than focusing on personalities, it deals with products, services, procedures, and how the work surrounding these factors should be completed. Operational conflict, when discussed logically by people with varied skills and perceptions, helps organizations produce optimal results.

In the most basic terms, interpersonal conflict is bad and operational conflict is good. Yet as we stated earlier, when properly managed, any type of conflict can be constructive. It is important to approach all differences in a collaborative manner and trace each conflict to its underlying cause. Although each problem that arises may be unique, most interpersonal conflicts are caused by biases and stereotypes. When corporations bring conflicts into the open, they are much more likely to constructively solve the problem and prevent it from recurring. However, in my many years in the consulting business I have met very few corporate managers who were willing to directly address the issue of stereotypes and biases. Instead, the vast majority of them responded with very vocal denials that conflicts in their companies had anything to do with those issues. It has become commonplace to lay blame on oversensitivity or overreaction. In the end, these managers dismiss, suppress, or cover up their companies problem until it ultimately surfaces in an explosive manner.

Compounding this problem of avoidance is the fact that widespread managerial denial creates an atmosphere in which the employees who are the victims of negative stereotyping are also reluctant to confront these issues. Given the current mood of many societies with regard to diversity, these individuals and groups simply will not express their true feelings about disparate treatment. To do so would only cause them to be branded as too sensitive and prone to overreaction. Any employee who receives this label feels that they are next to be booted out of the company, and justly so. In an environment like that, energies are very rarely geared toward productive work.

The Importance of Conflict Resolution

All humans struggle when dealing with conflict, but we all handle it in very different ways. Our reactions to conflict are often culturally motivated. On one side of the spectrum are certain Asian cultures in countries such as Japan, South Korea, and China in which members typically downplay conflict or try to avoid it at all costs. These tight-knit and racially homogeneous cultures place high value on consensus and agreement to ensure that everyone saves face. On the other side of the spectrum are certain African-American and some Latin cultures, which appear to be quite comfortable with direct conflict and believe that putting all matters on the table will lead to success. Between these two extremes are innumerable different and individual methods for dealing with conflict, and with each method often comes the belief that this is the right way to handle conflict.

If companies wish to resolve their diversity-related problems and all that accompany them, they must develop conflict resolution skills at each level of responsibility. One way to form diverse, high-performing teams is to teach managers and team members how to view conflict positively and use it constructively. Some of the potential benefits from positive conflict are as follows:

- Increased awareness of problems that exist and of the approaches to their solutions.
- Conscious consideration of problems and solutions, rather than suppression of them beneath the surface until they become extremely difficult to resolve.
- A greater awareness of injustices and discriminations, and a willingness to eliminate them.
- A heightened sensitivity toward the needs, values, and frustrations of others.
- The comfort to express opposing views, critique old reasoning processes, and develop new decision-making tools.
- Motivation for people to discover the roots of conflict, and openly assess what they find there.
- The creation of a dynamic atmosphere that promotes creative risk-taking.
- Improved morale and motivation, as employees feel empowered to make positive change in the company.
- Decrease in healthcare costs because employees are less stressed.
- Greatly increased skill levels for all workers.
- Increased efficiencies and decreased costs, made possible by dealing with problems directly and in a timely manner.
- Improved customer relations through a new awareness of their real needs and concerns.

- A reduction in the level of litigation against the company.

Simply avoiding conflict will not make it go away. Instead, conflict will begin to spill over into other areas of work and erode team cohesion. When employees feel uncomfortable, they tend to spend energy on staying out of sight, particularly during times of actual crisis, such as restructuring, downsizes, and mergers. Conflict avoidance is a big mistake in most situations, but particularly in relations with customers and stakeholders; it creates dissatisfied and disgruntled people who will eventually stop doing business with the firm. Leaders must develop strategies to constructively engage with dissatisfied customers and stakeholders in order to improve products and services and sustain organizational growth.

Ten Steps toward Conflict Resolution

We believe that the first conflict-management practice that organizations should implement is to view conflict as a healthy facet of today's work environment. This means creating an atmosphere where biases and stereotypes—especially regarding race, gender, religion, class, sexual orientation, ethnicity, age, and ability—can be discussed and explored rationally and productively. We realize that a number of readers believe this is easier said than done, but in actuality it is very methodic. Below, we have provided specific steps to help implement change. However, these cannot be effectively performed in the traditional bureaucratic organization. They can only be successful in the post-bureaucratic organization founded on Global-TREE^{SM}. We believe this should be the new model for the twenty-first century and beyond.

1. Whenever conflict arises, immediately acknowledge it. Try to describe and clarify the conflict, but don't try to immediately address it.

2. Find a suitable time and place to begin the conflict resolution process. Acknowledge the issues and allow the employees involved in the conflict enough time to process. This is extremely important, because it helps people avoid getting sidetracked when the real conversation begins.

3. At the second meeting, set up rules for the process and team behaviors. Focus on solving the conflict, not on attributing blame. Global-TREE^{SM} must drive all conversations. Everyone should be open and honest, have a voice, and be heard. Everyone should listen to each other without interruption, argument, or negative reaction. Attitudes need to be supportive and no one should rush to judgment. Questions should be open-ended and opinions and feelings should be supported by facts and specific behaviors. The conflict should be clearly defined in terms of what it is and what caused it.

4. Each person involved in the discussion should recognize the continuing cost of conflict and feel responsible for coming up with a mutually beneficial solution. Again, everyone must practice empathy and refuse to assign blame.

5. Everyone should employ the communication skills discussed later in Chapter 9.
6. Generate a number of possible solutions. Evaluate the positives and negatives of all solutions.
7. Agree upon the most appropriate solution and develop an action plan, then assign specific responsibilities for implementing it.
8. At every step in the process, team members should check in to share feelings about how the process is going.
9. Hold people to their commitments to successfully resolve the conflict.
10. Have a review process to assure that employees are working toward the solutions they committed to achieving. Make any adjustments as needed.

More than forty years of consulting and working within corporations have led me to one belief: many problems related to diversity arise from poor and ineffective—or completely nonexistent—communications and leadership. This has become the foundation for my hypotheses and I am certain that developing effective leadership characteristics and building effective communication skills are two of the greatest and most important challenges facing corporations and those who lead them.

Specific strategies are needed to teach employees the skills and behaviors needed to resolve conflicts productively. Corporations must encourage resolution of conflict and must clearly assist employees in understanding the negative effects associated with failing to deal with conflict in objective, open, direct, and timely ways. Those who are positive role models should be rewarded and celebrated. Those who are not there yet need to be educated, counseled, and given the opportunity to alter their behavior. If those employees cannot or do not change, they should be terminated.

The costs of poorly managed conflict are just as extreme and considerable as the costs of avoiding conflict. The benefits of productive conflict justify investment in conflict management skills, particularly related to issues of race, ethnicity, gender, classism, and sexual orientation. These methods should be used not only within the company, but with customers and stakeholders as well.

The Case Study

The challenges of forming diverse and high-performing teams are daunting and often seem insurmountable. We assure you, however, that this is not always the case. With commitment from the senior leadership and through the use of a multifaceted approach that focuses on each employee's self-awareness, it can be done. The following is a case study of an extremely dysfunctional high-level executive team. After using ARMC Global's holistic, inclusive team-building model, this organization's experience became a model for success.

The Situation:

A company heavily recruited a White male in his mid-thirties. He joined the company and performed very well for about a year. He was eventually promoted into a new unit as executive vice president (EVP). The business results from his new unit were just average, but the company needed significantly better results. This man's job was to turn that unit of the organization around.

He immediately began to encounter challenges with his new and fairly diverse team. Certain members believed they should have received the promotion that he got; others did not like the fact that the man came from a competitor company. The rest did not like his management style. After only six months, these issues grew into bigger problems. The situation deteriorated to such an extent that the company was ready to terminate the man's employment, but because of the significant investment they had made in him, they decided to hire ARMC Global to solve the problems.

The Assessment:

When approached by his senior leader, it became apparent that the executive did not want help because he believed he could solve the problems on his own. He believed that the problem was in his team and not in any way with him. Not surprisingly, most of the fourteen members of the team felt that if the executive were gone, everything would be fine. We have found this to be a typical and frequently occurring situation in many bureaucracies. The difference here is that the company was willing to try and resolve the situation without firing the executive. The success of that particular business unit was very important to the profitability of the company.

The Approach:

For this situation, a holistic approach focusing on team members' awareness of how life experiences impact values and behaviors was necessary. We knew that this approach would provide a much more complete picture of each team member. We used the following steps:

- Met with the senior leaders of the company to get their views about the situation, resulting in information about many other issues occurring within the team.
- After the meetings with senior leaders, ARMC Global met with the executive in question and his fourteen team members to conduct one-on-one interviews.
- From these interviews we developed a survey, with many of the questions drawn from information we gathered in the interviews. The survey focused on a number of areas including leadership; diversity; Proactive Inclusion®; the presence or absence of trust, respect, empathy, and ethics; career development plans; and living company values. We then administered the survey to the team members and their leader.
- Once the data was collected and analyzed, we met with the entire team and provided a detailed report with open-ended responses and statistical analysis. Then, we split the team into smaller groups based on our interviews. We asked them to analyze the data and come up

with the strengths and weaknesses of the team, as well as concrete solutions.

- There were low marks in many areas, specifically the areas related to trust, respect, empathy, and ethics. Many of the employees were afraid to voice their frustrations or concerns because they were worried about possible retaliation from leadership. This only exacerbated the root conflicts and made the employees believe that their leaders had hidden agendas designed only to advance their own careers. Additionally, the interviews found that twelve out of the fourteen team members were undermining the EVP, which caused further issues. The entire team was contributing to the problem.

- There was so much distrust and lack of respect that many members refused to discuss the results with the executive during the meeting. We insisted that he be part of the discussion to instill and reinforce the concept that this was a team effort and the leader was part of the team. We also coached the executive to listen more than speak, and to not get defensive. Through these efforts, ARMCG was able to facilitate a very constructive meeting with the leader and his team.

- After a complete discussion of the results, the team developed action steps and tasks to accomplish over the following two months. In addition, the team agreed to complete a series of 360-degree assessment tests that examine and evaluate behaviors. These assessment tools—the Leadership Styles Inventories (LSI)—assisted us in better identifying the problems and creating solutions to fix them. The LSI 1, a self-assessment, and the LSI 2, an external assessment of each person, provided insight into many of the team's problems. The members of the team had work styles that fell into non-constructive tendencies like defensiveness and intentional opposition. Team members also received low marks on the constructive leadership traits such as the ability to develop healthy relationships, ability to work effectively with people, and proficiency at accomplishing tasks.

- Not surprisingly, the results matched many of the characteristics of the ineffective teams. This was a critical situation.

- In conjunction with the LSI, ARMCG asked each member of the team, including the leader, to complete the Life Experiences and Values Inventory (LEVI) to help understand the reasons behind their particular work styles. The LEVI helps to identify a person's norms, values, and beliefs created largely by family, society, environment, and personal life experiences. It also helps employees to understand how these factors influence their interactions with individuals whose beliefs, values, and norms are very different from their own.

The Results:

In the follow-up meeting, held two months later, we gave concrete, constructive feedback to each person. We provided each team member with a complete report on his or her individual strengths and weaknesses, and recommended an action plan. With the exception of two, all the team members had begun to accept the fact that everyone was responsible for making changes. Each member was asked to provide the leader with an action plan and the team agreed on future steps with a follow-up session planned in two months to check team progress and discuss the LEVI results.

During the two months, the leader was mentored and coached by ARMCG and was required to present progress reports to ARMCG and the leaders of the company. Ultimately, the team lost the two members who were unable or unwilling to commit to positive change, but their departure enabled the team to come together and function much more effectively. After a year of successful work, the executive was given an award by the company for being the most changed and improved senior leader.

Conclusion

Increased innovation and better problem solving are often the chief benefits of utilizing high-performing teams composed of diverse individuals. However, before a team can start to work toward innovation, its members must develop a wide range of new skills and behavior patterns. A great deal of time, patience, and resources must be invested before anything can start to change. Trust, respect, empathy, and ethics have to be continuously fostered and each team member has to fully engage in the team-building process to develop relationships based upon GlobalTREE[SM].

By helping employees develop and implement teams, as well as holding them accountable for their work, corporations can avoid some major negative human tendencies. Corporations must begin by getting people excited about their work in teams, giving these teams real decision-making authority, rewarding team accomplishment significantly more than individual accomplishment, and structuring work in ways that are meaningful to all members of the team.

CHAPTER 8

The First Step Toward Change— Know Yourself!

"If we could change ourselves, the tendencies in the world would also change. As a man changes his own nature, so does the attitude of the world change towards him.... We need not wait to see what others do."

– Mahatma Gandhi

It seems abundantly clear to us that a new environment must be instituted in our organizations, and that environment is one in which GlobalTREE^{SM} is the guiding principle. In order for GlobalTREE^{SM} to spread throughout a company, employees must first gain insight into their own ideas, values, and perceptions; without such knowledge, the TREE can never fully take root. Leaders must realize that regardless of the structure and policies that are in place, a very specific strategy for reaching effective self-awareness and development is still needed. This strategy must help employees develop a deeper understanding about personal life experiences, human and genetic evolution, our brains' shortcomings, implicit and explicit biases, and natural tendencies to stereotype. This strategy must also be multi-faceted. It is obvious that we are complex specimens with multiple strengths and weaknesses; therefore, we must evaluate ourselves using a variety of tools in order to build an effective GlobalTREE^{SM}.

A productive GlobalTREE^{SM} environment requires that any hateful or derogatory thought, whether hidden or overt, is deemed unacceptable. People must be held to the highest level of personal accountability for their behaviors, their biases, their use of language, and their treatment of others, regardless of culture, ability, sexual orientation, gender, or ethnicity. When these standards are in place, trust, respect, empathy, and ethics can bloom.

Leading by Example: Change Occurs at Every Level

Regardless of an organization's size, mission, or leadership, a shift in attitude cannot occur unless each individual makes a conscious decision to change. The following quotes suggest how great thinkers have interpreted this truism over the centuries.

- "Let him that would move the world first move himself." – Socrates
- "He who cannot change the very fabric of his thought will never be able to change reality, and will never, therefore, make any progress." – Anwar Sadat

- "I change the world, the world changes me." –
  Libba Bray
- "We do not weave the web of life; we are merely
  a strand in it. Whatever we do to the web, we
  do to ourselves." – Chief Seattle
- "We don't accomplish anything in the world
  alone...and whatever happens is the result of
  the whole tapestry of one's life, all the weaving
  of individual threads from one to another, that
  creates something." – Sandra Day O'Connor

The first thing one must realize is that every employee is responsible for creating and maintaining an environment in which everyone feels safe, respected, and empowered to contribute to the fullest extent. However, the top leaders of corporations have the lion's share for making this environment possible. Leaders must act as role models for their employees and embody the appropriate values and behaviors for dealing with diverse populations. They must also be held accountable for their behavior during their performance evaluations, which will ensure that employees know that trust, respect, empathy, and ethics are valued by the company and are expected of all. Of course, there will always be a few employees who will resist and ignore leadership guidance. If that behavior persists, those employees should be let go. Allowing negativity to remain in the organization would be misleading and send the wrong message throughout the company.

Within a team, each member must hold one another accountable for creating and maintaining the healthiest working environment. It is imperative that all members speak up when a behavior or language inconsistent with GlobalTREE^{SM} is observed. At the team level, employees must coach each other and really commit to the development and personal growth of their team members, regardless of differences. Developing this environment is not easy, as many teams do not trust or respect the efforts of their peers. ARMC Global conducted research in ten business units throughout the world and found that employees tend to believe their coworkers are less likely to be as self-aware as they are. We asked participants to assess their level of agreement with the following statements, with 1 being "to no extent" and 10 being "to a great extent."

> **I periodically conduct a self-assessment to ensure that I understand my strengths and weaknesses. – 6.8**

> **Each team member periodically conducts a self-assessment to ensure he/she understands her/his own strengths and weaknesses. – 5.3**

These results contribute to the troubling trend of self-aggrandizement outlined throughout the book. As in other examples, employees gave themselves higher scores than their team members, but none of the scores suggest an extremely strong overall commitment to self-reflection. All employees must understand the value of self-assessment in the creation of GlobalTREE^{SM}. There is no room for the belief that a person in need of coaching is ignorant or incapable of change. The arrogance of those who refuse to accept the value in different viewpoints simply cannot exist within a productive organization.

Senior managers hold a particular responsibility for the culture in their organization because they have the power to develop strategies and champion behaviors needed to create GlobalTREE^{SM}. However, an organization's culture is not some sacred ideology that only leaders can affect or change. Organizational culture is the behavior that employees exhibit when they are not being observed. In a positive organizational culture, employees are ethical, empathetic, and inclusive when making decisions, working in teams, and performing their daily routines, even when no one is watching. These things are not only based on the corporate values that dominate an organization, but also on the values an employee brings to the company. Although the evolution of cultural change is often slow or at times even nonexistent, the very least one can do is change his or her personal thoughts and feelings in an attempt to improve and influence the thoughts and feelings of others. That alone is a great support to initiating change.

Emotional Intelligence

A positive emotional intelligence stems from a deep understanding of one's culture, biases, stereotypes, inefficiencies of the brain, strengths and weaknesses, and an awareness of how these factors influence our interactions and behaviors. The biggest problem organizations face regarding discrimination, poor morale, and conflict are due, in part, to the overall low emotional intelligence level of many employees. This, in turn, affects those employees with higher emotional intelligence levels, as they are adversely influenced by the negative culture around them. Raising a company's emotional intelligence level is a critical first step to creating world-class organizations based on GlobalTREE[SM].

Fortunately, corporations have recently begun to acknowledge the fact that employees bring many personal biases and prejudices into the workplace. Before this, during the 1950s into the 1980s, the prevailing attitude was that personal issues should not be brought to work; emotion was not a word that was even used in the corporate world. Throughout the 1990s, this attitude began to change, but a fully comprehensive and holistic approach never fully developed, and even today, many corporate employees still believe in that 1950s mindset. It is becoming clearer that human beings are incapable of leaving their personal issues and problems at home. Although some corporations are beginning to realize this, the number is too few. The corporations that do understand are the same ones that connect bottom-line benefits to an emotionally intelligent and diverse workforce that deals with diverse people empathetically.

Author and psychologist Daniel Goleman makes a strong case for why companies should pay more attention to emotional intelligence. "Imagine the benefits for work of being skilled in the basic emotional competencies—being attuned to the feelings of those we deal with, being able to handle disagreements so they do not escalate, having the ability to get into flow states while doing our work. Leadership is not domination, but the art of persuading people to work toward a common goal. And, in terms of managing our own career, there may be nothing more essential than recognizing our deepest feelings about what we do—and what changes might make us more truly satisfied with our work." Emotional intelligence is a vital employee trait, and to achieve this skill, each employee must conduct an honest self-assessment.

There are very few humans who really want to have greater self-awareness and self-knowledge. Most of us believe that our personal norms, values, assumptions, and behaviors are superior to others, and we fear continuous self-examination, worrying that we will find ourselves lacking. These emotions result in defiant denial of having any biases or stereotypes whatsoever. These beliefs become even more problematic when coupled with the incorrect notion that humans are rational and objective. Therefore, the necessary action is not finding ways to act rationally and objectively, but becoming aware of our subjectivity and irrationality. Those who acknowledge their shortcomings and sincerely attempt to resolve them are much more likely to perform effectively in environments with diverse teams.

Every human contributes to the problem, which means we can all become part of the solution. To do that, we must all work toward a higher level of emotional intelligence to change our attitudes and behaviors. As social psychologist Geert Hofstede observed, "Awareness is where it all starts: the recognition that I carry a particular mental software because of the way I was brought up, and that others, brought up in a different environment, carry a different software for equally good reasons." Without awareness, one runs the risk of walking through life ignorant about the situations and events that can change and develop a person. What is even more important is for businesses to realize the necessity of fostering this awareness in all of their employees.

To ensure success, employees will need some guidance, whether in business or personal matters, because managing our relationships is one of the hardest tasks humans confront. Interpersonal conflict is sure to arise when an individual feels a mismatch between his or her own expectations and those of another. It takes a high level of intellectual and emotional intelligence to view disconnects for what they generally are: simple conflicts in values or poor chemistry. But without any guidance on how to build one's emotional intelligence, employees are left in the dark. All too often, these employees will read too much into problems, blaming discrimination and unfair treatment as the cause. I would like to offer some guidance.

Self-Assessment Tools

You are a complex being. As you seek better self-awareness, it is important to make use of several possible approaches that can lead you to the most comprehensive understanding of yourself. Several of these approaches are listed and explained over the next few pages.

The Life Experiences and Value Inventory (LEVI)

The first challenge in becoming self-aware is to identify the norms, values, and beliefs created by our families, environments, and life experiences. Then we need to understand how these factors influence our interactions with individuals whose norms, values, and beliefs differ from ours. With this clearer perception, we can develop better solutions and strategies to deal with cultural interactions and issues at both professional and personal levels.

To help employees understand the diversity issues they face, ARMC Global has developed the Life Experiences and Value Inventory (LEVI). Participants are asked to fill out a survey with questions about themselves in areas such as geography, family structure, religion, language, or socioeconomic status. Examples of topics and questions are listed below.

- **Gender**
    1. In your family, what expectations/roles were set for boys/men? For girls/women?
    2. What, if any, norms, values, and beliefs did you adopt as a result of your gender or of your family's expectations for boys/men and girls/women?
    3. In what ways, if at all, do these norms, values, and beliefs guide your behavior in your personal and work life?
    4. What changes would you like to, and/or do you think you should, make in your norms, values, and beliefs with regard to gender, so as to become better able to work with and to influence different race, gender, and ethnic groups?

- **Race/Ethnicity**
    1. With which racial/ethnic group do you most identity?

2. What advantages, if any, have you gained because of your race/ethnicity?
3. What obstacles, if any, have you encountered because of your race/ethnicity?
4. How have these obstacles/advantages impacted your professional life?
5. Describe the first time that you interacted with someone of a different racial/ethnic group.
6. Was this a positive, negative, or neutral experience, and how so?
7. What conclusions, if any, did you draw about this racial/ethnic group from that first experience of it?
8. What types of words/stereotypes/descriptions did you/do you hear frequently about your own racial/ethnic group?
    A. As a child?
    B. Today?
9. How, if at all, has your race/ethnicity shaped your norms, values, and beliefs?
10. How have your interactions with people of different racial/ethnic groups shaped your norms, values, and beliefs?
11. How do those norms, values, and beliefs impact your:
    A. Personal life?
    B. Work life?
12. Please describe, using as much detail as you can, other ways in which your race/ethnicity has impacted you.

- **Significant Life Events**

  Besides the demographic characteristics mentioned, we know that significant life events can also greatly impact how we see the world and interact with others. Thus, the LEVI ends with the following questions:

  1. What significant life events—such as geographic moves, job changes, changes in financial status or socioeconomic class, health issues, death of a loved one, divorce, and birth of children—have impacted your norms, values, beliefs, and behaviors?

  2. Please describe what you consider to be your most life-changing event(s) and the impact they had on you personally and/or professionally.

Many people who have taken the LEVI have spoken to us about its incredible usefulness. The assessment works particularly well if the participant shares his or her LEVI results with the rest of their team. The only way to bring about change is to begin with oneself and work outward, taking into account all of those whom you affect.

Emotional Intelligence Assessment

Although corporate leaders have just begun to recognize the significance of emotional intelligence, they're not really focused on this crucial concept despite the fact that psychologists and social scientists have been trying to understand and measure emotional intelligence for a long time.

Social psychologist Reuven Bar-On developed the Emotional Intelligence Assessment, which measures "an assortment of fifteen different capabilities, competencies and skills that influence one's ability to succeed in coping with environmental demands and pressures, and directly affect one's overall psychological well-being." The questions on Bar-On's assessment use validity scales to ensure the participant gives open and honest responses, which are then grouped into five major categories in the scoring system. These categories are listed and explained below.

1. Intrapersonal: includes emotional self-awareness, assertiveness, self-regard, self-actualization, and independence.
2. Interpersonal: includes empathy, skills in interpersonal relationships, and social responsibility.
3. Adaptability: involves problem solving, flexibility, and reality testing.
4. Stress Management: covers the ability to handle stress and to control impulses.
5. General Mood: includes overall happiness.

Over nine thousand people around the world have used this instrument, and researchers discovered that emotional intelligence levels fall into consistent patterns across all cultures. According to the results, "The same high score traits common to successful people in North America were also found among successful individuals in Nigeria, India, Argentina, and France. And along with culture, there were no differences between genders either."

Psychoanalysis

For further self-assessment, psychoanalysis or some other type of professionally guided introspection can be useful. This form of self-assessment requires an objective third-party individual to guide the process. However, be sure to do a careful comparison of the professional's training and experience with his or her own LEVI results. Doing this will help determine if there are any significant contrasting views that will hinder the process and create barriers in working together toward a positive outcome.

Inside and Outside Assessment

ARMCG's final recommendation is to have trusted confidants, both inside and outside of the organization, who can help serve as sounding boards for your perceptions and feelings. We particularly stress confiding in those outside your organization because they will most likely have a better idea of how your personal characteristics could impact work issues. They're also unlikely to be influenced by your particular corporate environment.

Another helpful assessment is the 360-degree Leadership WorkStyles (LWS). This works in very similar ways to the Leadership Styles Inventory (LSI) discussed in Chapter 7. Beyond helping those in a direct leadership role, it can be very beneficial by further explaining tendencies and behaviors in all business situations.

Every self-analysis method has its strengths and weaknesses, but by adopting multiple types of self-assessment one can compile the most holistic, thorough, and useful feedback. And although the heaviest responsibility for self-analysis should be placed on the individual, organizations must encourage, assist, and hold everyone accountable. Those days of denying the effects of employees' psychological characteristics are long gone.

Fourteen Necessary Skills for Success in Multicultural Environments

To help you begin your own self-assessments and avoid common mistakes, ARMCG has highlighted the skills needed to operate effectively in multicultural environments. The Society for Intercultural Education Training and Research (SIETAR) has identified fourteen of the most important of those skills and presented them so that each one builds on the others. The first seven skills are internal, dealing with self-awareness and our ability to understand and acknowledge our stereotypes. Once the first seven skills are developed, one can move on to the remaining seven, which are external and help us interact effectively with people of different cultural backgrounds. Each one helps build a stronger emotional intelligence by bringing to the surface conscious thoughts about particular strengths and weaknesses.

1. *Know your own culture (values, beliefs, assumptions).*
2. *Know your own limitations (strengths and weaknesses).*
3. *Practice empathy with others.*

4. *Respect other cultures.*
5. *Learn by interacting.*
6. *Strive to be nonjudgmental.*
7. *Be aware of your stereotypes.*
8. *Learn how to communicate effectively and compassionately.*
9. *Listen closely, and observe carefully.*
10. *Strive to relate meaningfully to those you perceive as "different."*
11. *Be flexible: Learn how to adapt.*
12. *Adjust yourself according to people's reactions.*
13. *Learn how to live with ambiguity.*
14. *Be as consistent as you can be without becoming inflexible.*

Along with these characteristics, each skill is broken down and defined to help you truly understand their meanings. You will also find recommended actions to achieve these skills. Each skill is extremely important in relation to the others and to our ability to understand ourselves.

1. Know Your Own Culture

As explained throughout this book, culture encompasses our values, beliefs, and assumptions as well as characteristics like age or race. We use this as a lens to view and judge our world and the people inside it. Since we base our behaviors on this viewpoint, we must be totally aware of it to effectively interact with a wide range of cultures. The following are some suggestions to help raise awareness.

- Reflect on early life experiences and significant emotional events that have shaped your value systems, beliefs, and attitudes. Try to understand formative influences such as family structure, socioeconomic status, and religion. Assessments like the Life Experiences and Values Inventory (LEVI) and the Leadership WorkStyles (LWS) are useful instruments.
- Keep a journal in which you carefully note reactions to current world events and news reports. Analyze and discuss these reactions with others.
- Enroll in courses that examine and discuss cultures, values, and beliefs.
- Learn as much as you can from other people in your own culture.
- Take part in group discussions.
- Participate in activities relevant to your culture.
- Read material that examines your culture, especially material that outlines your culture's origins, history, and norms; avoid one-sided ideas.

2. Know Your Own Limitations

In order to maximize strengths and minimize weaknesses, we must accept their existence. Only then can we identify them and begin to understand how they help or harm us in our daily lives. Below are behaviors that can heighten awareness of your own strengths and weaknesses.

- Broaden your perspective on what factors have influenced the norms, values, and beliefs that you hold. Make sure to explore all potential influences, such as race, gender, education, religious beliefs, or age.

- Request feedback from multiple sources about your strengths and weaknesses. Ask people who will be truly honest and make sure to really listen to what they say. Try to get this information from people who are different from you in areas of culture, socioeconomic status, or sexual orientation.

- Seek experiences that enable you to practice your strengths and diminish your weaknesses.

- Change the things about yourself that you can and accept what you cannot or do not wish to change. After making this decision, be very aware of its consequences.

3. Practice Empathy with Others

To be empathetic means to identify and understand the situations, feelings, and motives of others. The ability to see the world from another's perspective is a powerful one, and we can never fully comprehend that perspective unless there is a deep understanding of both of the previous skills listed above: knowing your own culture and knowing your limitations. Here are some strategies to help build empathy:

- Develop relationships with as many people from as many diverse backgrounds as you can, not only at work but outside of work as well.

- Listen closely to the views of your friends and acquaintances and work hard to understand them, especially if theirs greatly differ from your own.
- Help friends and acquaintances in any efforts and goals they are embarking upon or trying to accomplish.
- Join organizations that help advance the interests of cultures other than your own.
- Consciously decide to live in a community with a lot of diversity.

4. Respect Other Cultures

Generally, those who do not strive to understand or appreciate other cultures, and those who view differences as wrong or weird, are those who do not respect other cultures. Consider the following steps in order to establish and maintain respect for those who are not like you.

- Cultivate friendships with people from many different cultures.
- Do not judge cultural differences. One person's values are not necessarily better or worse than another's, but simply reflect the culture.
- Continually question your judgments of others by recognizing that they have different behaviors.
- Attend cultural events to strengthen your understanding of their histories and origins.

- Learn another language and travel to other countries.
- Learn as much as you can about different cultures by taking courses or reading books.

5. Learn by Interacting

Sharing interactions and experiences with people of different cultural backgrounds gives us new perspectives and allows us to rethink our assumptions and hopefully eliminate our stereotypes. Here is a list of suggestions to help accomplish this:

- Join associations that deal specifically with the concerns of different races, genders, ages, religions, and sexual orientations.
- Join organizations that work toward healing the injustices committed against groups with which you identify and groups other than your own.
- Pay close attention to the way others react to your behavior.
- If you don't understand those reactions and the reasons behind them, ask for clarification and pay attention to the responses in a non-judgmental manner.
- Delve more deeply into the customs, languages, and behaviors of others whom you find puzzling.
- If possible, spend some time living in another country.

6. Strive to Be Nonjudgmental

Being completely nonjudgmental is a huge challenge because so many of us have been subconsciously socialized to believe that our culture is right and superior to other cultures. The following advice can help you resist the temptation to form instant impressions and be less judgmental.

- Keep in mind that our brains make snap judgments. You need to be aware of this trait and work hard to get past this roadblock to objectivity.
- Remember that your culture is only one standard among many when it comes to assessing norms and values.
- Strive to consistently maintain a positive and open attitude.
- Acknowledge that our snap judgments about events or people affect our next encounter with them.
- Remember that your perceptions can sometimes be true, but many times they are not. One way to be nonjudgmental is to question your perceptions to make sure they are correct.
- Recognize that sometimes we become so focused on one aspect of a person or situation that we miss seeing the whole picture.
- If you have formed a negative opinion about someone, look for ways to prove yourself wrong.

7. Be Aware of Your Stereotypes

Stereotyping is normal, but also extremely dangerous because it inevitably leads to misinterpretation, unresolved conflicts, and organizational ineffectiveness. Listed below are some ways to increase your awareness of your stereotypes.

- Work to understand the dynamics of your conflicts with others instead of merely pretending friction does not exist.
- Understand that while the brain does automatically stereotype, we each have the opportunity to acknowledge that fact and then do something about it.
- Develop relationships with people from diverse backgrounds to help break down any stereotypes that you may have.
- Enter into learning situations where stereotypes are openly identified and confronted.
- Take stereotyping exercises such as First Thoughts or the Implicit Association Test on the Harvard University website. These tests analyze the first thoughts that come to mind when we hear certain words.

8. Learn How to Communicate Effectively and Compassionately

Relationships with people from diverse backgrounds and cultures are fragile and can easily be derailed by poor communication. As we attempt to exchange ideas through speech, writing, and signals, our messages can very easily become garbled. This lack of understanding often leads to conflict and can ultimately result in discrimination and unfair treatment. The following suggestions are ways to strengthen your communication skills. Chapter Nine discusses these ideas at length.

- Recognize that 85 percent of our communication is nonverbal, which is difficult to control.
- Practice speaking directly, candidly, clearly, tactfully, and compassionately.
- Practice active listening, which means paraphrasing what the other person has said and checking with them to make sure your interpretations are accurate.
- Constantly assess your perceptions by asking if your interpretations of behaviors and nonverbal signals have been valid.
- Ask people who were present but did not participate in the conversation to give you feedback.
- Study the communication skills and styles of many different cultures.

9. Listen Closely, and Observe Carefully

This particular skill requires you to stop obsessing over personal concerns and ideas and tune in to the thoughts and feelings of others. This not only allows you to listen and observe better, but also helps you to build greater respect for other cultures and people (Skill 4). Listed below are tips to help improve your listening ability.

- Develop more effective communication skills (see Chapter 9).
- Ask probing questions to help distinguish between what someone has actually expressed and your own reactions.
- Instead of making statements that place blame on others, consider using less accusatory and confrontational words and including yourself as part of the problem.
- Ask people you trust to confront you in situations when you only appear to be listening, but really are not.
- Talk less; think and listen more.
- Develop your ability to observe by taking part in workshops where trained facilitators give you immediate feedback on your level of awareness.
- Have honest discussions with people you trust and respect from backgrounds other than your own.

10. Strive to Relate Meaningfully to Those You Perceive as "Different"

It is absolutely necessary to build relationships with a variety of groups and individuals who have different needs and goals from your own. Listed below are tips to help improve your relationship skills.

- Recognize that everyone in an organization must constantly work to understand, value, respect, and appreciate the differences in background, culture, and value systems within the organization in order for it to become world class.
- Understand that each employee has skills different from your own. If you can recognize and respect those differences, you will find that their skills are often complementary to yours.
- Remember that our differences only mean our backgrounds differ, not our potential.
- Make a point to build relationships with people you originally classified as different.

11. Be Flexible: Learn How to Adapt

The diversity in today's global environment demands that we all be multicultural. This means we must improve our ability to adapt to the environments in which we live and work, and refrain from imposing our value systems on others. To do this, consider trying out the following ideas.

- Spend time with people from diverse cultures, inside and outside of work.
- Know what your strongest skills are and benefit from working with individuals who have complementary skills.
- Consciously seek out information and experiences related to different cultures and peoples

to expand your range of thoughts, ideas, and options.

- Read publications that express different viewpoints from your own.
- Travel so you can experience other peoples and cultures in their own surroundings.
- Become actively involved in groups and organizations that will not always allow you to get your way.

12. Adjust Yourself According to People's Reactions

When trying to develop a team or influence others, it is extremely important to read your audience's reactions correctly. You can adjust certain behaviors to produce a beneficial outcome to all if doing so is practical and ethical. In order to improve your ability to read others, take into account the following ideas.

- Solicit feedback on yourself from as many different sources as possible.
- Adjust your behavior in response to that feedback, and then request more feedback on those adjustments.
- Do not take offense to negative reactions; instead, try to learn and grow from them by communicating empathetically.
- Intentionally place yourself in situations where you may be disagreed with or reacted to negatively in order to improve your responses.

13. Learn How to Live with Ambiguity

No one knows everything about all cultures. Nor can we all cope perfectly with the unavoidable stress of uncertainty and ambiguity that go along with living in our multicultural world. The following are tips to help deal with that stress and discomfort.

- Seek out situations that induce discomfort and then discover the best ways to raise your comfort level.
- Solicit guidance from a diverse group of people for appropriate behaviors when you find yourself in ambiguous circumstances.
- Continually push beyond the boundaries that your lifestyle and your worldview have trained you to expect.

14. Be as Consistent as You Can Be without Becoming Inflexible

Being consistent does not mean acting the same way all the time, but rather consistently treating people fairly, justly, and reasonably according to their unique needs. Solicit feedback from a variety of people, both at work and outside of work, who have had a chance to observe you in widely varying situations.

- Participate in training sessions that provide you with opportunities to deal with unfamiliar situations.

Conclusion

The first step toward creating GlobalTREE^{SM} is to have leaders who epitomize the values of trust, respect, empathy, and ethics. The second step is to encourage each employee to conduct an accurate and honest self-assessment to allow him or her to positively contribute to that environment. We all have unresolved psychological issues; so much of our psychological makeup was developed in childhood, it is difficult to fully understand what makes us tick. Yet, if employees and their leaders are to prosper in a global arena, they have no choice but to discover their true selves. It is crucial that organizations not only require self-assessment, but also provide their employees with the tools to foster awareness of themselves and of others.

CHAPTER 9

Creating Healthy Communication Among Diverse Employees

"So when you are listening to somebody, completely, attentively, then you are listening not only to the words, but also to the feeling of what is being conveyed, to the whole of it, not part of it."

— Jiddu Krishnamurti

We all claim to understand the importance of healthy communication, but when we are under the strain of life's complexities and in the heat of business interactions, we rarely give much thought to the overwhelming significance of what effective communicating actually means. The ability to communicate well is the building block for moving with ease through life, but most humans find it difficult. Consider how hard it can be to maintain good communications within your immediate family. It is no wonder that effective communication is so rare in the workplace.

Effective communication is crucial to our Global-TREE[SM] strategy to move beyond the rhetoric of meritocracies. We believe that the communication skills of employees in today's corporations have deteriorated despite all the technology to keep us connected and all the efforts and emphasis that corporations place on improving communications. Communication breakdowns are one of the major roadblocks to building successful businesses because they affect every aspect of operations.

One of the most damaging effects of poor communication skills is decreased workplace productivity. If employees are bogged down by ineffective communication patterns or if they are distracted by communication conflicts, they are not focused on the task at hand. When conflicts occur as a result of ineffective communication, the workplace loses trust, respect, and empathy, and more issues arise around ethics issues. These factors will only worsen in more diverse workplaces if leaders do not recognize the impact different cultures can have on communications. And finally, poor communication skills often affect customer satisfaction. Many customers have negative perceptions about customer service due to bad past experiences, so it is not surprising that they communicate expecting the worst. Customer service employees take the brunt of that negativity, and often react with hostility. In the end, all parties involved are upset and inevitably feel wronged, when the entire situation could have been remedied through communications based on GlobalTREE[SM].

In previous chapters, I recommended examining personal values, strengths, and weaknesses in order to improve your communication skills, but there is more work to be done. In this chapter, I present the key barriers that prevent effective communication, especially among people from different backgrounds, as well as tools to help immediately establish good communication.

Factors That Deter Healthy Communication

In our work at ARMC Global helping organizations, it no longer surprises us to find that many of their problems are caused by communication breakdowns. After exploring these issues further, we have noticed a few common traits. The first is that employees are denied access to pertinent information, which causes them to spend extra time on assignments and to behave in ways that are incompatible with organizational and team values. When information is not shared in a timely, accurate, and honest manner, conflict inevitably occurs. These factors lead to products and services that do not meet world-class standards.

Another factor making communication difficult is that regardless of cultural background, most of us possess a natural shyness when interacting with those outside of our close circles. Generally, we hold back much of what we really think and try to avoid making our issues and frustrations public. When these thoughts and frustrations finally surface, voicing them in a calm and productive way is difficult. This situation is further complicated when those frustrations are personal in nature. When misunderstandings and grievances fester beneath the surface, they can pollute the entire workplace.

The final—and perhaps most destructive—trend is defensiveness. Employees who are insecure about their performance, the stability of their position, or their status in the company will act defensively, effectively barring any feedback or differing opinions from influencing their behavior. The following list is comprised of three common reasons we have found for people's defensive tendencies:

1. Humans tend to cherish their opinions; disagreements with others make us feel attacked or vulnerable, which in turn causes us to be overzealous when defending our positions.

2. In disagreements, we do not hear what the other person is really saying, but we rather note the fact of disagreement and immediately start to respond with, "Yeah, but…" That disagreement naturally disappoints and frustrates us.

3. We are deeply bothered by our inability to clearly articulate our views. We project that frustration onto the listener and interpret his or her puzzled reaction as hostile, resulting in negative feelings all around.

Communication in a GlobalTREE℠ Environment

The keys to communication lie within the establishment of trust, respect, empathy, and ethics among all employees. You will build trust when you follow through on your promises and do what you say you will. Respect is an essential requirement in engaging with coworkers. Empathy will allow you to understand other people's perspectives and communicate in a way that promotes understanding. Finally, committing to a sense of ethics will ensure that your communications are straightforward, direct, and without hidden agendas or personal biases.

A GlobalTREE℠ environment is also one in which everyone is proud of their contributions to the company's success, is able to communicate concerns or suggest improvements, and is willing to simply learn about what others do within their organization. Leaders in these environments have also led by example. When leaders break down communication barriers and exemplify trust, respect, empathy, and ethics, their behavior becomes a model for the entire company. Establishing GlobalTREE℠ is a great first step in improving communications, but there is still more work to be done.

Healthy Communication vs. Unhealthy Communication

Most workplaces can nourish open and honest communication. They simply need to focus on these efforts. ARMC Global has identified eight attitudes and behaviors that contribute to healthy communication and eight behaviors and attitudes that lead to unhealthy communication. Consider the differences below between defensive climates and supportive climates that enhance cooperative and constructive communication.

Unhealthy Defensive Traits	Healthy Supportive Traits
* Partial Listening	* Holistic Listening
* Indirect Communication	* Direct Communication
* Overly Hasty Evaluation	* Patient and Fair Evaluation
* Desire for Control	* Collaboration
* Strategy	* Spontaneity
* Neutrality	* Empathy
* Superiority	* Equality
* Arrogant Certainty	* Mellow Provisionalism

To help clarify these traits, each is described in detail, which will help readers in working toward the healthy behaviors and avoiding the negative ones. Each trait is based on the establishment of mutual GlobalTREE^{SM} among individuals.

Partial versus Holistic Listening

To listen holistically means to not only hear the words being said, but to also observe all of the nonverbal types of communication. Holistic listeners, unlike partial listeners, realize that nonverbal cues can actually contradict the message of spoken words. Although the speaker may use words that signify understanding or acceptance, body language may indicate disagreement. Generally speaking, body language reveals actual feelings.

Indirect versus Direct Communication

In many cultures people rarely verbalize what they truly mean, therefore communication becomes indirect or cryptic, and often results in vague and misinterpreted messages. We can significantly improve our communications if we simply say exactly what we mean, but do so in a way that is highly respectful and sensitive to others.

Overly Hasty versus Patient and Fair Evaluation

Judgmental communications, whether verbal or nonverbal, will very often be lost on the recipient. Adding to the problem is the fact that many cultural groups blame, label, or question others based solely on a dogmatic belief in their own superiority. Communications can be open, straightforward, and honest without creating defensiveness, as long as it is descriptive instead of judgmental. It should simply and soberly state facts rather than being overly emotional or accusatory.

Desire for Control versus Collaboration

Many of our human interactions focus on persuasion: influencing behaviors, changing attitudes, or curtailing the activities of others. This focus persists despite knowing that we succeed best when our intent is to collaborate and not exert control.

Strategy versus Spontaneity

When interacting, if people believe there is a hidden agenda or see the speaker as playing an insincere role, they will become resentful and defensive. Yet when information and its sources are simply and freely shared, an atmosphere of trust, respect, empathy, and ethics is created. This also allows all team members to feel valued.

Neutrality versus Empathy

When we identify and understand other people's problems and feelings while accepting their emotional reactions, even if we perceive them as excessive or hostile, we reassure them and increase productivity. Yet when we blatantly deny the legitimacy of the emotions of others, we create a closed and hostile environment. This breeds hurt feelings, low productivity, and the possible charge of discrimination.

Superiority versus Equality

When we convey a sense of superiority over others, we inevitably set off their defense mechanisms. The resulting feelings of inadequacy cause people to listen only to their emotions, subsequently creating resentment that will greatly affect communications.

Arrogant Certainty versus Mellow Provisionalism

A person displaying arrogant certainty knows all the answers, requires no additional information, and holds him- or herself as the ultimate authority. This communication style of this kind of person will probably cause others discomfort. Wiser communicators interact with mellow provisionalism, viewing their own thoughts and ideas as in transition instead of permanent. In allowing different ideas to influence your thinking, you open up the possibility for new and innovative thought.

How Diverse Cultures Impact Communication

The problems with defensive behavior and other negative communication patterns become particularly troublesome when interactions occur between people of different cultures. The following ten common barriers to communication can be found in any organization, but are especially prevalent with highly diverse populations. Read through the following list and recall if and when you have personally come into contact with them. Reflect on how you felt and how you handled the situation.

1. Different languages, and even different regions that speak the same language, have different uses and meanings for the same word.
2. Each word may have many different meanings in one language.
3. One language may not have words to clearly express a concept that is common in another language.
4. There are clashes in communication styles among different cultures.
5. There are numerous forms and styles of non-verbal communication.
6. Everyone is guilty of implicit and explicit stereotyping.
7. Making snap judgments in conversations and not really listening to what is being said is common.
8. Our brains play cognitive tricks on us.
9. Most of us have some anxiety or personal discomfort, especially when significant organizational change occurs.
10. There is a degree of awkwardness and apprehension in communicating with people who are different from us.

Almost all of today's corporations employ people from various backgrounds. These differences can cause managers to be at odds with employees, employees to be at odds with customers, and everyone to be at odds with stakeholders—obviously a very negative working environment. Simply put, the people involved in a conflict often blame a simple

misunderstanding on some deep-rooted stereotype or bias
and pass the entire thing off as discrimination and unfair
treatment. Also, if a conflict has a potentially controversial
component such as race, ethnicity, gender, or sexual orientation, humans avoid it, speaking indirectly while using
qualifiers and euphemisms. This subtlety and indirection,
however politely intended, almost always leads to incorrect
assumptions and miscommunications, which in turn lead to
more conflict and unhealthy relationships. Add these com-
plications to the variety of ways we have been socialized in
different cultures, and it is easy to see how difficult communicating can be.

Consider the following hypothetical situation to understand the possible consequences of this type of negative
environment. A male manager hates giving employee feedback on job performance; he believes he doesn't do it very
well and would rather not speak directly to an employee
whom he believes is working below par. The manager
believes it is far better to avoid making a scene and hopes
the problem will just resolve itself. At his company, a
female employee believes that she is doing a great job, but
the manager considers her performance barely adequate.
The manager says nothing until her performance review
when his real opinion is finally revealed. The employee is
deeply disappointed by her negative appraisal and, having
no prior information, alleges unfair treatment, which in
turn upsets the manager. In this atmosphere, now poisoned
and completely lacking trust and respect, it is very possible
that the employee will believe she received her low evalu-
ation because of her age, looks, ethnicity, gender, sexual
orientation, or some other identity factor. She may feel

that she has no other recourse than to contact an attorney to file a discrimination suit. This is only one example of how these types of interactions can take place. As explained previously, customers can very easily fall victim to this miscommunication as well, with disastrous impact to the bottom line. It is very easy to become ensnared in these types of situations, but they are also just as easy to avoid by being aware of warning signs.

Effective Communication in Diverse Groups: Non-Verbal Factors, Verbal Cues, and Holistic Listening

While we all must work to improve our communication skills no matter what our work environment is like, those who work with people from a variety of different cultures must take extra care to ensure healthy communication. At ARMC Global, we believe that communication is only 15 percent verbal, while 85 percent is nonverbal. Given this ratio, an effective communicator must pay the most attention to such nonverbal factors as eye contact, body language, tone, interpersonal distance, and volume of voice. Factors like race, ethnicity, culture, gender, and class affect the nonverbal signals we send to each other when we communicate with each other. For example, people from the Middle East are accustomed to having very little personal space when they engage in conversation. By contrast, Northern Europeans leave more space and may feel uncomfortable if someone speaks to them from only six inches away. It's quite possible that a male Middle Eastern manager working alongside a female Northern European employee will create the perception of sexual harassment purely because of cultural norms. Or consider a White, middle-class person from the Midwest of the United States observing a group of Cubans in Miami having a heated discussion about politics. With voices raised, hands flying, and personal space invaded, the White observer could interpret the scene as a vicious argument when in reality it is a friendly discussion.

Although these examples show how significant body language is, words will always be extremely important. In order to communicate effectively, the words used must hold the same meaning for the speaker as they do for the listener. Yet in English alone, linguists have estimated that the five hundred most often-used words can produce more than fourteen thousand meanings. To further complicate things, the meanings of each of those words generally have a direct correlation to an individual's cultural experiences and background. The greater the dissimilarity of those experiences, the less likely it is that the speaker and listener attach the same meaning to the words. One example of this is the word "babe," often used by men and women alike in certain contexts as a term for "pal" or "buddy." In the corporate world, if a man uses "babe" in any context, it would be no surprise to find him quickly facing complaint and a visit from human resources. In Philadelphia, Pennsylvania's Italian Market, the word "babe" is normal and acceptable language; in fact, if you react negatively, most people in the market would wonder what is wrong with you.

Paying attention to non-verbal cues and making sure all parties understand the meaning of language used in conversation will certainly help interactions go more smoothly, but we can also work on our listening skills. The goal of holistic listening is to hear and understand all of what a person is communicating while providing empathetic understanding. It requires a specific way of hearing in which the listener reflects the information heard back to the speaker, and refrains from analyzing, interpreting, or judging what was said. This is a difficult concept for most of us because we have a natural tendency to evaluate, approve, disapprove, or make judgments based on what we hear. However, as long as we are aware of these tendencies, we can work to change them.

In order to achieve holistic listening, we need to really commit to understanding what the other person intends to communicate. We can do this by asking ourselves the following questions:

- What is the person speaking committed to?
- What, if any, are his or her concerns?
- What am I supposed to take away from this conversation?
- Do I understand what the other person is trying to say?

As we practice these steps toward holistic listening, we will find ourselves listening in a whole new way. We will be listening for commitments, concerns, and, most importantly, for understanding.

The final piece of advice for communicating in diverse environments is to be aware of cultural nuances, including your own. To minimize misinterpretations, it is important to appreciate the different customs of cultures other than your own. In order to influence others, we must communicate effectively, which means ensuring our message is accurately heard. The following list provides some specific tips for making communications direct, clear, and concise regardless of where or with whom one is speaking.

- Address all communication problems directly and in an empathetic fashion, rather than pretending they do not exist.
- Avoid using qualifiers that reinforce stereotypes.
- Avoid jargon and keep your message simple.
- Use a wide variety of analogies, metaphors, and references to make your point clear to a wide variety of audiences.
- Addressing one's own shortcomings when giving criticism and developing solutions is an assertive way of expressing unhappiness while respecting those with whom you are working.
- In some circumstances, using a demonstration to aid in explanation can reinforce your message faster than mere words.
- Constantly be aware of your nonverbal cues, as well as those of others.
- If you sense that you're not being understood, repeat yourself using different words. Ask questions frequently to see if your message is being communicated effectively.
- Make sure your questions are direct, concise, clear, and do not force a specific answer.
- Make sure you completely understand the responses you receive and that they fully answer your question.

- Find ways to acknowledge and affirm the speaker's emotional state. Strive to pick up on nonverbal cues.
- Summarize your conversation before concluding to ensure that everyone has arrived at the same understanding of what was said.
- Always follow up conversations in writing to confirm discussions and agreements and to avoid repetition.
- Admit confusion and lack of clarity and actively decide to reach answers together. Honest acknowledgment of uncertainty helps convey sincerity.
- Give the speaker your complete attention. Encourage them to openly share more thoughts and ideas.
- Understand that each one of us has our own agenda to help us achieve our goals and protect ourselves. Don't assume that someone will know or share your agenda, so discuss what is important to you and to others to build a solid foundation for mutual understanding and communication.

Characteristics of Effective Feedback

One of the most important types of communication in the workplace is feedback. It allows employees to know where they stand as performers, to receive career counseling, and to develop in the most effective ways possible. It also helps employees continuously upgrade their knowledge and skills, changing behavior where needed. Feedback gives information about which behaviors are effective and whether the message actually reaches listeners. The ultimate goal of giving and receiving feedback is to build trust, respect, and empathy between employees and managers in order to foster an environment that produces the best work. This can all be achieved with the right communication techniques.

In order for feedback to be most effective, it must be shared at the right moment. Relaxed surroundings and sufficient time for complete discussion are vital for any good feedback session. Feedback should never be given when one is under stress, including being busy, hungry, angry, or tired. Nothing good will come out of feedback if any of the people involved are not at their most receptive.

The specific focus of the session should be on the task and the behavior, not on the person. A manager's feedback should spotlight specific shortcomings in the behavior of the employee so that he or she may improve or change them. Good feedback confines itself to an employee's actual behaviors without attempting to judge them. Companies often forget that feedback also needs to be given for positive actions and not just when improvement is needed. This is very important because employees will strive harder to produce good work if they feel appreciated.

It is also crucial that feedback be a give-and-take process. The person giving the feedback must be an active listener and continuously make sure the recipient understands the message. It is also extremely important that managers take into account the needs, concerns, and desires of their

employees, otherwise feedback can easily be taken negatively, disregarded, or resented. After feedback sessions, it
is imperative to check back in to ensure the message was
given and received accurately. At that point, steps can be
taken to either continue or further improve behaviors.

There are numerous books, articles, and seminars that
discuss how to give feedback, but I feel that one of the best
was written by the National Training Laboratories Institute
(NTL). For specific ways to improve feedback, the following tips were taken directly from the NTL's *Reading Book for
Human Relations Training*:

Effective Feedback	Ineffective Feedback
Describes the behavior that led to the feedback: "You are finishing my sentences for me."	Uses evaluation/judgmental statements: "You're being rude." Or generalized ones: "You're trying to control the conversation."
Comes as soon as appropriate after the behavior—immediately if possible. Later if events make it necessary, if you need time to cool down, if the person has other feedback to deal with, etc.	Is delayed, saved up, and "dumped." Also known as "gunny-sacking" or ambushing. Induces guilt and anger in the receiver, because after time has passed there's usually not much he or she can do about it.
Is direct, from sender to receiver.	Is indirect or ricocheted ("Tom, how do you feel when Jim cracks his knuckles?").
Is "owned" by the sender, who uses "I" messages and takes responsibility for his or her thoughts, feelings, and reactions.	"Ownership" is transferred to "people," "the book," "upper management," "everybody," "we," "they," etc.

(continued on next page)

(continued from previous page)

Effective Feedback	Ineffective Feedback
Includes the sender's real feelings about the behavior, insofar as they are relevant to the feedback: "I get frustrated when I'm trying to make a point and you keep finishing my sentences."	Feelings are concealed, misrepresented, distorted. One way to do this is to "transfer ownership." Another way is to hide the feelings by being sarcastic, sulking, competing to see who's "right," etc. Other indicators: speculations on the receiver's intentions ("You're trying to drive me nuts"), motivations ("You're just trying to see how much you can get away with"), or psychological "problems" ("You have a need to get even with the world").
Is checked for clarity to ensure that the receiver fully understands what's being conveyed. "Do you understand what I mean when I say you seem to be sending me a double message?"	Is not checked. Sender either assumes clarity or—fairly often—is not interested in whether the receiver understands fully: "Stop interrupting me with 'Yes, buts'!"
Asks relevant questions that seek information (have a problem-solving quality), with the receiver knowing why the information is sought and having a clear sense that the sender does not know the answer.	Asks questions that are really statements ("Do you think I'm going to let you get away with that?") or that sound like traps ("How many times have you been late this week?"). Experts at the "question game" can easily combine the two ("How do you think that makes me feel?").

Effective Feedback	Ineffective Feedback
Specifies consequences of the behavior—present and/ or future ("When you finish my sentences, I get frustrated and want to stop talking with you," or "If you keep finishing my sentences, I won't want to spend much time talking with you in the future.").	Provides vague consequences ("That kind of behavior is going to get you into trouble.") or specifies no consequences, instead substituting other kinds of leverage, such as "should" ("You shouldn't do that.").
Refers to behaviors about which one can *do* something ("I wish you'd stop interrupting me.").	Refers to behaviors over which the receiver has little or no control, if he or she is to remain authentic ("I wish you'd laugh at my jokes.").
Takes into account the needs of both sender and receiver; recognizes that this is a "process," that this is an interaction in which, at any moment, the sender can become the receiver. (Sender: "I'm getting frustrated by the fact that often you're not ready to leave when I am." Receiver: "I know that's a problem, and I'm concerned about what seems to be your need to have me always do *what* you want, *when* you want.")	Is distorted by the sender's needs (usually unconscious or unconsidered) to be safe ("Now I don't want you to get angry, but..."), to punish ("Ah-ha, then you admit you do interrupt me?"), to be virtuous ("I'm going to level with you, be open with you..."), etc. In short, most ineffective feedback behaviors come from the sender not seeing the process as an interaction in which both parties have needs that must be taken into account.

(continued on next page)

(continued from previous page)

Effective Feedback	Ineffective Feedback
Affirms the receiver's existence and worth by acknowledging his or her "right" to have the reactions she or he has, whatever they may be, and shows willingness to work through issues in a game-free way.	Denies or discounts the receiver by using statistics, abstractions, and averages or by refusing to accept his or her feelings ("Oh you're just being paranoid," "Come on! You're overreacting," or "You're not really as angry as you say you are.").
Acknowledges and, when necessary, makes use of the fact that a process is going on, that it needs to be monitored, and sometimes explored and improved. ("I'm getting the impression that we're not listening to each other. I'd like to talk about that and try to do this more effectively.")	Either does not value the concept of "process" or does not want to take time to discuss anything other than content. Consequently, does not pay attention to the process, which can result in confusion, wasted time and energy, and lots of ineffective feedback.

Conclusion

To build the most effective companies with the most productive teams, good communication is a crucial step. Not only because it helps build a proactively inclusive environment based on GlobalTREE[SM], but also because it allows for innovation and truly fosters growth in people, teams, and corporations. Although establishing good communication is not easy to accomplish and takes sincere dedication and constant awareness of the barriers that will inevitably arise, at ARMCG we know that it can be done. To have truly effective communications, each of us must understand who we are as individuals and how our unique norms, values, and cultures affect our behaviors. Only by understanding ourselves can we understand our communication strengths and weaknesses. We have provided a number of ways to increase healthy communication, but the most important advice we can give is to continue to improve your communication skills, whether your goal is to provide more effective feedback, improve your ability to listen, or to bring more clarity and precision to your messages.

CHAPTER 10

Key Reminders for Becoming a Great 21st Century Leader

"The characteristics of tomorrow's great leaders will be an ability to stand firmly between a myriad of conflicting demands and balance the needs of themselves, their followers and the wider world and time to provide a leadership that inspires changes that a post-capitalist world will require."

– Anonymous,
from Windsor Leadership Trust meeting

In the nearly four decades during which I have been hired to coach, train, and develop leaders, I have learned as much as I have taught. While I have emphasized that leadership starts with a commitment to understanding and improving oneself, at ARMC Global we have found that many organizations are not willing to spend the time, effort, or money to allow employees at all levels to invest in education for this purpose. I have taught that human nature, human evolution, and human biology are complex subjects that we must all acquaint ourselves with in order to function effectively and with minimal conflict in the workplace. But I have learned too often that many organizations pretend that humans are all the same and that we are able to suppress our individuality, our emotions, and our subjectivities when we come to work each day. And while I have taught that in order to build effective, world-class teams leaders must focus on trust, respect, empathy, and ethics among their employees, I have found that many leaders prefer to focus on technical, administrative, and professional skills instead.

However, one of the greatest lessons we have learned at ARMCG is that individuals, leaders, organizations, and societies can change. We have entered many situations where these ideas were met with resistance and even hostility, but with steady, dedicated attention to Proactive Inclusion and GlobalTREE^{SM}, these situations were reversed. We have found that when leaders and organizations fail to solve their problems it is often because they have pre-conceived notions about leadership that they learned at business school, in the media, or from their own leaders in the workplace. We believe there must be a shift in the way we understand leadership, as evidenced in recent years by the many examples of leaders guided by short-term financial gains, self-centeredness, greed, and arrogance. We believe this shift must occur in the media, in our educational system, in our families, in our political institutions, in our businesses, and in society as a whole.

One major example of how we must adjust our ideas around leadership can be found in the very popular competency frameworks that many organizations use today to assess their employees. As outlined throughout this book, leadership is complex and dynamic. Unfortunately, most businesses are looking for a quick fix for the issues they face, so they evaluate leaders in ways that simplify what leadership really is. The competency framework approach has become one of the most dominant models of management and leadership assessment and development. While the apparent objectivity and "scientific" nature of competency frameworks remains highly attractive as a means for measuring, assessing, and developing managers and leaders, it is not without faults and can even produce misleading results.

Richard Bolden and Jonathan Gosling of Exeter University and the Centre for Leadership Studies in the United Kingdom have studied the history, uses, and drawbacks of competency frameworks for a number of years. In 2004, they studied the research of the Windsor Leadership Trust (WLT), a leading non-profit designed to highlight emerging and innovative leadership ideas identified through experience, research, and dialogue. From 2001 to 2004, WLT solicited feedback from a wide variety of leaders and managers at all levels about the nature of leadership. Bolden and Gosling compared these findings to their own research in 2003 on leadership competency and quality frameworks from twenty-nine international and U.K. organizations from a wide range of industries. Bolden and Gosling's landmark study found that many of the characteristics, values, traits, and abilities that WLT found essential for good leadership were not present in many competency frameworks. For example, in more than one third of the competency frameworks, concepts like personal values and vision were not included as important qualities for leadership. Inspiration, flexibility, resilience, adaptability, trust, and ethics were absent from two thirds of the competency frameworks. And a shocking 80 percent of competency frameworks did not include emotional intelligence, moral courage, personal beliefs, personal reflection, coping with complexity, or work-life balance.

Clearly, most competency frameworks lack some of the key characteristics needed to be effective leaders, and what is worse, many companies rely primarily on these assessments to identify who is fit to lead, where leadership gaps lie, and how to address these gaps. As a result, these organizations create leaders who lack the most important skills needed to build teams: trust, respect, empathy, and ethics. Furthermore, they fail to understand one very important lesson: good leadership is not constant or static; it is complex, fluid, and varies depending on the situation.

Essentially, there is no quick path to excellent leadership. Anyone who is interested in becoming a better leader must commit to a lifetime of learning. I hope that this book is a helpful step for those who seek to become better leaders. I know that any one leadership skill or quality I have written about, like confidence, empathy, communication skills, or innovative thinking, won't work alone. Leaders must be able to analyze which skills are needed for each situation, based on their own experience and their knowledge of the individuals and circumstances involved. I believe the key insights I have provided can help leaders in their analyses.

Review of Key Insights

Leaders are not adequately prepared for the rapidly changing, complex problems businesses face today and will continue to face in the twenty-first century. These problems are not only technical and financial but also political and social. The key to facing these issues is adopting the key leadership skills that humans have valued throughout civilization: the ability to improve themselves, selflessness, generosity, fairness, and compassion. These were the leadership traits that ensured survival in small hunter-gatherer tribes.

The world has greatly changed, but humans still appreciate these values, much more than the current leadership trends such as short-term focus, greed, and self-centeredness. These tendencies have resulted in executives amassing enormous personal wealth, while their employees struggle to accumulate any wealth at all. In the United States, the wealthiest 20 percent of households own approximately 80 percent of privately held wealth, and the poorest 80 percent share the remaining 20 percent. Leaders today could better serve their organizations if they could better appreciate how these significant differences in wealth distribution are affecting our global economy and our societies.

We should not minimize the differences between cultures, races, ethnicities, and genders, but it is clear that there are baseline ideals that all humans want: trust, respect, empathy, and ethics. Advanced Research Management Consultants Global (ARMCG) has created the GlobalTREE^{SM} system, which we have introduced successfully for more than twenty years in our consulting work with organizations, corporations, and universities as they strived to create an environment in which all types of people can be productive, effective, and respected.

ARMCG also developed Proactive Inclusion®, a strategy based on GlobalTREE℠ that was designed to help organizations hire, retain, and fully utilize the best talent, skills, and ideas available to serve increasingly diverse and demanding constituencies. Whether organizations conduct business in countries around the world or only in one small town, they all must understand the impact of an increasingly interconnected human population. By recognizing and valuing the diversity of employees' unique backgrounds and proficiencies, organizations that commit to Proactive Inclusion® will be prepared to meet the needs of a constantly changing business landscape. Adoption of Global-TREE℠ and Proactive Inclusion® will enable companies to anticipate and more effectively respond to changing social, political, and economic conditions, and to take advantage of emerging markets, products, and services around the world.

Before leaders can move toward effectively changing the environment of the workplace they must first understand the basics of human evolution, both cultural and genetic. It is important that leaders appreciate that our cultural evolution has developed much faster than our biological evolution. The human brain today is similar to our brain of tens of thousands of years ago, but the daily routines and practices of our cultures scarcely resemble those of ancient times. And so, while we consider ourselves quite advanced, the human brain still falls short in a number of ways. We tend to use shortcuts in our process of identification, which result in stereotypes and biases of those who are not like us, and trigger us to favor our kin or "pseudo kin," those who are most similar to us.

To eliminate hurtful biases and stereotypes, we must acknowledge their existence, attempt to understand why humans use them, and realize how harmful they can be. As previously outlined, we tend to think of ourselves as objective and fair; we've created constitutions and laws that uphold ideals of equality, non-discrimination, and justice. But in reality, concepts like racism and sexism are cultural ideologies that position the powerful group as being inherently superior to groups that are marginalized. We have also seen throughout the world that when these ideals are held by a large enough group of people, they become engrained in the society, at both an individual and institutional level. When this occurs, it becomes possible for the group in power to perpetuate these beliefs in order to maintain their position of power.

Leaders in the twenty-first century must face the challenge of understanding culture and its complexities. Culture is made up of three important factors: religion, language, and ethnicity. Leaders must recognize that each person is a unique cultural human being. More specifically, each of these factors does not affect a person's identity in the same way. We are all individuals whose unique experiences determine how we relate to our own cultural identities.

As humans and our cultures have evolved, so have our institutions. Bureaucracy was born thousands of years ago out of a need to organize and conduct commerce equitably among newly developing agricultural societies, and that the hierarchical systems would help build efficient industrial companies and technological societies. However, bureaucracy has not kept pace with rapidly changing employee populations. Workers are more educated and less interested in being cogs in the machine. To be successful, twenty-first-century leaders must adjust their organizations to meet the needs and desires of an ever-changing, diverse workforce. These leaders must also solve some major issues facing today's bureaucracies: dehumanized workforce, politics, homogeneity, lack of flexibility, misuse of knowledge, and lack of innovation.

As leaders build more diverse and less homogenous teams, they will find improved efficiency and innovation, but they may also find more conflict. The ability to openly and constructively deal with conflict is an essential skill for all leaders, despite the fact that most of us would like to avoid conflict entirely. But we know that when conflict festers beneath the surface it can become very destructive when it finally erupts, sometimes causing negative publicity, lost business, reduced productivity, poor customer service, low morale, wasted energy, and missed opportunities. One of the most important concepts to understand is that poor leadership is often a major source of disruption. Leaders can make significant and positive changes in the workplace by looking inward and developing a strong sense of awareness and emotional intelligence.

It is important that all employees understand their own values and ideas, but it is up to the leader to begin this process. Leaders must set the tone for the kind of behavior that is appropriate and acceptable, and to do that, they must have a high degree of self-awareness so that they can understand their own biases, stereotypes, and other shortcomings. Leaders must exhibit emotional intelligence, although

getting companies to understand the importance of emotion is not always easy. For decades, businesses preferred to
believe it was possible to leave emotions and personal issues
at home. While many now realize that this is an unrealistic
expectation, few companies really work to develop those
skills in their employees. The companies that do develop
those skills realize that an emotionally intelligent workforce will better be able to form diverse, high-performance
teams because they are able to deal with diverse customers
empathetically and compassionately, a skill that will ultimately help the bottom line.

Once employees have cultivated a strong sense of self-
awareness, they will be better equipped to make improvements in another important area that is absolutely crucial
but difficult for high-performance teams: communication.
Most companies can work to develop healthy communication; they must simply make that effort a priority. In order
to help make this process easier, I have outlined the characteristics of healthy communication versus unhealthy communication. I have also described the strength of holistic
listening and the importance of paying attention to verbal
clues. These skills are particularly important in diverse
environments, as cultural differences can create confusion
for those who assume that everyone shares their own cultural norms.

Three Essential Reminders

If you have reached this point in the book, you have probably realized that becoming an effective, world-class leader
is a complex endeavor. The requirements, along with the

situations, technologies, and consumers, are constantly shifting, and I hope that if you have learned one thing from this book it is that becoming a good leader is a dynamic and ongoing process. I realize that I have presented a lot of information, so I have identified three major points to keep in mind. Although many leadership competency frameworks have left out these important qualities, in thirty years of working with corporations, universities, non-profits, and small businesses, ARMC Global has seen these three qualities in the most successful leaders: an understanding of human nature, an understanding of self, and a commitment to trust, respect, empathy, and ethics.

The best leaders understand humans. Not just how to deal with their fellow employees, but how humans have evolved, how our brains function, how our environments shape our beliefs, and how we create and maintain stereotypes and biases. The better a leader understands humans, the better he or she is at creating an atmosphere in which all of the diverse members of a team can work together effectively, handle conflict constructively, and face the many inter-personal challenges that will surely arise. Leaders who take the time to understand human nature will be able to appreciate and celebrate all of the varied and unique ways that humans look, sound, behave, and live their lives, all while realizing that at a base level we all share the same needs and desires.

The best leaders understand themselves. They have taken the idea of learning about humans to the next level. They realize that each human is a reflection of his or her genealogy, their environments throughout their lives, their unique experiences, and their distinct, subjective perspectives. When leaders take the time to understand who they really are and why they think the way they do, they open themselves up to a new realm of possibilities, in the workplace and in their personal lives. In acknowledging and seeking out the sources of their biases and stereotypes, these leaders find they are better able to understand those who are different from them. In exploring who they really are, they become more confident in their moral compass, their goals, and their vision for the future. And in realizing that they are only human, like the rest of us, they are better able to communicate with a broad spectrum of people.

Finally, the best leaders recognize that they must commit to building trust, respect, empathy, and ethics in their organizations. Having heightened their own emotional intelligence, successful leaders realize that without significant, continuous, multifaceted investment in building the emotional intelligence of their people, they will not be able to significantly minimize the negative effects of human subjectivities and shortcomings that create tremendous inefficiencies in organizations and societies. These leaders understand that in order to gain a competitive edge in our increasingly interconnected world, their organizations must be able to attract, hire, and retain the best candidates from around the globe, from every culture, language, race, ethnicity, gender, age group, and religious background. These leaders have successfully advocated that their organizations value their diverse and varied workforce as their most important asset, going to great lengths in order to ensure that each team member is valued, heard, trusted, utilized, accepted, and respected.

My colleagues at ARMC Global and I strongly believe that if you understand humans, understand yourself, and commit to fostering trust, respect, empathy, and ethics through GlobalTREE^{SM}, you will be an effective leader in any situation. Leadership is something that must be continuously improved and this is true now more than ever. As more and more political leaders are disgraced for corrupt backroom dealings, as corporate leaders are bankrupting their businesses, and as leaders in all sectors are found exploiting their positions of power, we hope that society is finally ready to shift the understanding of what it takes to lead. And we hope that you are ready to take the first steps to exemplify a new model of leadership.

Acknowledgments

I must acknowledge Dr. Valarie Molaison and Laura Stiffler, who contributed significantly to the initial stages of this book.

Malia Bruker has done a great job not only on editing but also with providing excellent critique and input. Her valuable support over the past months has been absolutely crucial in all phases of publishing. Liz Lyman did a critical and wonderful job copyediting, despite her extremely busy schedule.

Erin Hart has been by my side from page one and without her tremendous support in many areas, this book would not be finished. Dr. Wesley Collier has also been extremely supportive throughout the process of creating this work and his multiple talents have been invaluable to me. Ben Johnson has been an employee, friend, and ally for more than twenty years. His support throughout this process has been vital.

A special note of thanks to Dr. Mahzarin Banaji for her brilliant concepts, which have greatly influenced my creative thinking.

About the Author

Dr. John P. Fernandez received his B.A. magna cum laude from Harvard University and his Ph.D. from the University of California–Berkeley.

A leader with AT&T for fifteen years, Dr. Fernandez held division-level managerial positions in operations, labor relations, and human resources. He is the president of ARMC Global, a full-service human resources consulting firm he founded in 1983. John taught at Yale University, University of Pennsylvania, New York University, and Antioch University. He is the author of ten cutting-edge books related to diversity, leadership, teambuilding, competitiveness in a global marketplace, childcare, and elder care.

Index

Aamodt, Sandra, 61

Advanced Research Management Consultants Global (ARMCG), 4, 7, 15, 18, 26, 29, 35, 40, 44, 51, 68, 74, 83, 100, 114-115, 117, 147, 164, 187-188, 198, 203, 208, 224, 227, 233, 245, 254, 256

Advancement, 130, 156, 178; lack of, 51, 53

Affirmative action, 43

Africa, 51, 107, 109, 111-112

African Americans, 83, 89

African-Caribbean, 84

African cultures, 106

African descent, 52

Agriculture, 15, 23, 50, 102, 127-128

Allman, John, 57

American Indian, 110. *See also* Native American

Annan, Kofi, 67

Argentina, 207

ARMC Global. *See* Advanced Research Management Consultants Global

Asian 86, 106, 107, 113-114; cultures, 106, 182

Attention blindness, 62, 93

Attitude(s), 70, 72, 81, 87, 95, 116-117, 124, 144, 185, 195, 196, 200-201, 210, 214, 227; changing, 229; generational based, 153; Machiavellian, 149; negative implicit, 92; positive implicit, 92; racial, 90-92; sexist, 133

Australia, 109, 113, 122

Bar-on, Reven, 206

Banaji, Mahzarin, 82-83, 86, 92

Bateson, Mary Catherine, 163

Behaviors, discriminatory, 68

Belgium, 107

Beliefs, 13-14, 18, 19, 29, 50, 52, 69-70, 81, 93, 95, 102-103, 105, 106-107, 116, 121-124, 191, 201, 202-205, 209-211, 254

Biases and Stereotypes, 81-83, 99, 184, 251; beauty, 90; cognitive tools or cultural weapons, 68-72; gender, 87; group, 87-92; race, 88-89; skin color, 90-91; in action, 85-86; implicit, 19, 47, 80; implicit and explicit, 2, 6-7, 64, 67-97; minimizing, 13; nature of, 84-85; natural tendency, 73-74; overcoming, 81-82; prevalence of, 93; supporting data for skeptics, 82-92; weight, 86. *See also* stereotype

Black(s): blacks, 69, 84, 85-86; dark-skinned, 91; doll, 89; faces, 89; first black President, 53; girls, 88-89; light-skinned, 91; man, 106; males ,69; patient,86; percentage of population, 113-114; skin, 89; sounding names, 89; T-shirt, 62

Body language, 228

Bolden, Richard, 33-35, 247, 248

Brain, human, 36, 65, 82, 89, 92-95, 140, 161, 168, 254; characteristics of, 2, 68; evolution of, 56-61; plays tricks, 6, 61-64, 231, 250; short comings and strengths of, 7, 9-12, 19, 36, 99, 196, 199; snap judgments, 214, tendency to stereotype, 73-74, 215

Brazil, 27, 44, 69, 106, 113, 122; Brazilian, 12, 14, 78

Buddhism, 115, 121-123

Buffett, Warren, 21, 29

Bulgaria, 107
Bureaucracy, 16, 126-161
Business: business units, 164-165,
    198; business unit preferences, 12

Calcification, 140-144
Cambridge University, 115
Canada, 44, 113, 122
Cape Verdean, 114
Career, 83, 130, 134, 145, 156, 178,
    189, 200, 237
Castelli, Luigi, 90
Caterpillar, 27
Catholic, 114, 122- 123
Center for Leadership Studies at
    University of Exeter, 33
Change, case for, 135-138
China, 106-107, 111-113, 122, 130,
    182
Chinese, 71, 76, 84-85, 106, 118;
    managers, 121; traditional religion,
    121
Christianity, 53, 121-123
Chrysler/Mercedes, 17
Clark, Kenneth, 88
Climates: defensive, 227; supportive,
    227
Cognitive tricks, 6, 36, 61, 62, 95, 232
Communication(s), 103, 120, 137,
    158, 171, 177, 186; diverse cultures
    and, 230-237; factors that deter
    healthy communication, 225-226;
    healthy versus unhealthy, 224-230,
    unhealthy, 19
Communication conflicts, 3, 8, 19,
    124, 136, 156-158, 172, 177-178,
    185, 216-217, 224, 223-243
Competency frameworks, 20, 33-35,
    247-248, 254
Conduct: codes of, 159; unethical, 20
Conflicts, 5-7, 17, 97; addressing
    inherent conflicts, 30-33; between
    organizations and people; 42-43;
    community, 24; complex, 1-2;
    conflict case study, 187-192;
    constructive, 159, 175, 180-184;
    constructively dealing with, 174;
    genocidal, 111; 119, importance
    of resolution, 182-184; in

bureaucracies, 15-16,135-136, 152;
    managing, 180-192, organizational
    conflicts, 30-33; ten steps to resolve,
    184-187
Conformity, 47, 152
Corporate strategy, 7, 45-47. *See also*
    Proactive Inclusion
Costco, 28
Culture: and biases, 69; backgrounds,
    15, 19, 213, 225; change, 40, 53,
    199; clashes, 16-17, 163-193;
    complexities, 37; complexity and
    subjectivity of, 99-125; conflicts,
    99, 101; differences, 102, 114,
    119, 124, 160, 212, 253; evolution,
    3,9, 36, 49, 52-55; explicit values,
    102-103; group(s), 14-15, 68, 103,
    108, 117, 124, 228; growth, 10;
    identity, 13-14, 111, 116, 121, 124;
    ideologies, 68, 251; irrational, 104-
    105, issues, 3; norms, 104, 107,
    234; nuances, 14-15, 105-108, 118,
    235; values, 14, 110; unhealthy, 17;
    weapons, 68
Cunningham, William A., 89
Customers, 26, 144; cultural needs of,
    101; dissatisfied, 136-137; diverse,
    46, 118, 142, 144, 147, 151, 153,
    155-160, 174, 176, 178, 180, 183-
    184, 224, 231, 233, 252-253

Daniel Goleman, 200-201
Dartmouth University, 85
Deutsche post, 27
Discrimination, 68, 72, 216;
    blaming, 202, 232; charge of, 229;
    consequences of, 80; eliminating,
    35; education about, 68,72; in
    resumes, 88; (law) suit, 233;
    positive, 43; reverse, 44, unfair
    treatment and, 202, 216, 232
Distrust: avoiding, 20, 46-48, 82, 158,
    173-174, 221; and bias, 99; and
    communication, 224, 226-227; of
    coworkers, 146, 150; and feedback,
    238; and leadership, 3, 26-27,
    34, 77, 164, 170, 177, 179, 190,
    196-198, 246, 248-249, 254-256;
    assessment, 167

Diversity, 1, 3-4, 9, 22, 35, 41, 43-44, 96, 100, 114, 116, 158, 160, 161, 174, 176, 182, 186, 189, 212, 218, 250, 259

East India, 79, 114
Empathy, 3, 7-8, 16, 20, 22, 27, 36-37, 41, 46, 49, 57, 82, 92, 100, 102, 119, 125, 139, 146, 150, 158, 164, 167, 177, 189-190, 193, 196, 221, 224, 227, 229, 238, 246, 248-249, 254-256
Employee(s), 45-47, 108, 125, 130, 132-134, 164, 168-170, 174-175, 193, 195-203, 208, 218, 221; bureaucracy and, 136-138, 142-163; communication and, 19, 223-225, 231-233; conflict and, 17, 31, 42-43, 100-101; culture and, 106, 116-120, 123; feedback and, 237-238; leaders and, 2, 6-9, 22, 25-29, 37, 172, 177-187, 190-191, 245-247, 249-250, 252-254; stereotypes and, 12-13
Ethics, 3, 7-8, 16, 20, 22, 27, 34, 36-37, 41, 43, 46, 49, 57, 82, 92, 100, 102, 117, 119, 125, 139, 146, 150, 158,164, 165, 167, 177, 189-190, 193, 196-197, 221, 224, 226-227, 229, 246, 248-249, 254-256
Ethical, 19, 22, 24, 34, 103, 167, 199, 219, 221
Ethnicity, 8, 13, 52, 90, 95, 104, 110-114, 121, 180, 187, 196, 203-204, 232-233, 251; culture and, 110-115; identity and, 109, 112-115
Ethnocentric assumptions, 70
Europe, 109; eastern, 111; people in, 26, 104, 113; heritage in, 110, 112; northern, 233
European Union, 44, 119
Evolution: biological, 9-10, 51-53, 65; cultural, 3, 9, 36, 49, 52-55, human, 50-51; processes of, 3; psychology, 59, 65, 154; speed, 9, 59
Explicit biases, 2, 6, 11-13, 33, 36, 46, 64, 67-68, 89-90, 140; culture and, 124; overcoming, 81-84, 92-94, 156, 196

Feedback, 18, 95-96, 156, 161, 210; constructive, 192, 208, 211, 216-227, 219-220; effective, 237-243; inaccurate, 178-179; ineffective, 237-243
Finland, 107, 112
France, 27, 107, 119, 206; people of, 14, 75, 113, 119-120
Ferguson, Kathy, 137

Gandhi, Mahatma, 21, 195
Gates, Bill, 29
Genes, 31, 51-53, 55-56, 64
Genetics 49, 54-56; versus culture, 54-56
Germany, 27, 53, 70, 107, 112-113, 122, 129
Gestalt, 63
GlobalTREE, 7-9, 16, 18-20, 22, 27, 30, 35-36, 39-47, 49, 54, 57, 82, 92, 96, 100, 102, 126, 133, 146, 155-156, 158-161, 164-178, 193, 195-196, 199, 200, 221, 224, 226-228, 242, 246, 250, 256
Goleman, Daniel, 200-201

Harrison, Matthew S., 91
Harvard Business Review, 7
Harvard Implicit Association Test (IAT), 13, 83
Harvard University, 82, 85, 114-115, 259
Health, 50, 100; and environment, 41, 95, 167; issues of, 203; mental, 12, 77, 138-139; organizational, 30; professionals, 88; public, 114; and relationships, 6, 148, 151, 191; seeking assistance for, 77, services, 12
Heitmeyer, Wilhelm, 70-72
Hierarchies, 15, 31, 127-162
Hindi, 14
Hinduism, 121
Hispanic/Latino, 76, 114
History, 127-132
Hofstede, Geert, 104,201
Holistic approach, 189, 200
Holistic listening, 227-228, 233, 235, 253

Homogeneity, 151-153
Homophobia, 11, 41, 68, 107
Human beings, 5-6, 8, 12, 15-16, 37, 43, 46, 51, 55, 64, 74, 109, 136, 140, 168, 200, 251
Human subjectivity, 92, 96; what we can do, 92-97
Humanize, how to, 138-140

Ideal (the), 132-135
Immigration: unfair laws, 71, 103, status of, 110
Implicit bias: age, 91; assumptions, 81-82, 93; insidious, 71; racial, 85-86, 89, 91; assessment, 88
Innovation, 20, 40, 42, 47, 143, 145-149, 158-159, 192, 242, 252
Iran, 113, 122
Islam, 53, 121-123
Italy, 90, 112

Japan, 27, 61, 107-108, 112, 115, 119-120, 129-130, 182; people of, 12, 69, 77, 104, 108, 113, 115, 117-119
Jews, 12, 71, 75, 84, 85-86, 123
Journal of General Internal Medicine, 86

Kim, Do-Yeong, 83
Korea: people of, 14, 69, 83; South, 109, 182
Krishnamurti, Jiddu, 223

Language, 8, 13, 19, 53, 55, 59, 67, 90, 95, 101, 112-114, 116-121, 158, 169, 180, 196, 198, 203, 213; body language, 228, 233, 234
Lay, Kenneth, 26
Leadership, 2-3, 5, 10-11, 13, 20, 28-37, 39-45, 47-55, 57-73, 71-82, 87, 108, 147, 152, 159, 163-164, 168, 173, 186-187, 196, 197, 207, 210, 254, 256, 259; assessment, 246-248; case study, 187-192; guiding principles of, 158-161; history of, 21-25; new model of, 24, 33, 44, 154-161, 185; poor, 29-30, 252; role of the leader, 177-193; state of, 24-29; training, 31-34, 246

Leadership Styles Inventories (LSI), 191, 207
Leadership WorkStyles (LWS), 207, 210
Levi, 18, 191-192, 202-203, 205, 207, 210
Libet, Benjamin, 60
Listening, 19, 144, 174, 216-217, 223, 226-228, 233-235, 242, 253
Lynch, Dina, 180
Lucnt/Actel, 17

Madoff, Bernie, 26
Malaysia, 44, 71
Manager(s), 3, 21, 26-27, 32-35, 80, 83, 102, 118, 180-182, 199, 231, 232-233, 238, 247
Mannheim, Karl, 138
Martin, Trayvon, 69
Mead, Margaret, 39
Men, 69, 76-77, 83, 86, 87, 111, 114-115, 141, 188, 195, 234
Mentors, 7, 35
Merit, 74, 130, 132, 141
Meritocracy, 132-133
Merton, Robert, 141,
Middle East, 107, 111; people of, 69, 106, 233
Mill, John Stuart, 127
Minorities, 72, 113
MIT, 87
Multicultural environments, 18, 118, 208, 218
Multicultural world, 220
Muslim(s), 12, 14, 80, 122-123
Myth of objectivity, 74-81

National Training Laboratories (NTL) Institute, 239
Native American, 117
New Zealand, 109
Nigeria, 112-113, 116, 122, 206; people of, 12, 79, 112
North America, 110, 206
Northern Ireland, 69, 111

Oh, Hye-Jung, 83
Ohio State University, 89
Organization, 3, 200

Overweight, 12, 78, 88

People of color, 14, 84
Performance appraisals, 45
Personal space, 116, 233-234
Pettigrew, Thomas, 138-139
Poland, 107
Politicians, 13, 77
Politics, 115, 147-151, 158, 161
Portugal, 112; people of, 78, 114
Positional power, 132-133, 162
Prezzolini, Giuseppe, 141
Proactive Inclusion, 7-9, 18, 39-47,
    82, 96, 158-159, 189, 250
Psychoanalysis, 207

Race, 8, 13, 18, 44, 52, 67, 80, 83,
    88, 90, 95, 104, 112, 114-115, 150,
    184, 203-204, 209, 211, 213, 232-
    233, 249, 255
Racism, 11, 41, 68-70, 105, 152, 161,
    251
Recognition, 36, 42, 45, 74, 106, 109,
    128, 176, 201
Relationships: healthy, 6, 148, 191;
    unhealthy, 151, 232
Religion(s), 8, 13, 18, 67-69, 80, 82,
    95, 97, 103-104, 112-114, 121—
    124, 160, 184, 203, 210, 251
Respect, 3, 7-8, 16, 20, 22, 27, 36-37,
    41, 43, 45-46, 49, 54, 57, 82, 92,
    100, 102, 107-108, 119, 125, 136,
    139, 146, 150, 156, 158, 164, 167,
    173, 177, 189-100, 193, 196-198,
    212, 216-218, 221, 224, 227-229,
    232, 238, 246, 248-249, 254-256
Rules, 140-144; calcification of, 140-144
Russell, Bertrand, 99
Russia, 73, 113, 123
Rutgers University, 85

Satellite, 155
Saudi Arabia, 54, 69, 106
Self-awareness, 5, 28, 32, 46, 185,
    195, 201-202, 208, 252
Sexism, 11, 41, 68-70, 152, 161, 251
Sexual harassment, 234
Sexual orientation, 9, 95, 103, 160,
    184, 186, 187, 196, 211, 213

Shinto, 115
Siemens, 27
Silo, 149, 150
Sinegal, James, 28
Skills, 1-2, 4-6, 8, 9-15, 17-22, 26,
    35-36, 52, 88, 125, 143, 158, 171,
    173, 181-182, 186-187, 192, 206,
    208-209, 216-218, 224, 233-234,
    243, 246, 248-250, 253
Skin color, 83, 90-91
Social Cognition, 91
Society, 1, 13, 23, 52, 54, 55, 69, 72,
    103, 104, 105, 108, 119, 120, 128,
    129, 131, 135-136, 191, 251
Society for International Education
    Training and Research, 208
Sony, 27
South Africans, 79
South America, 111, 114
Spain, 112-123
Spanish, 110, 113-114, 120
Spencer, Steven J., 85
Stereotypes, 11-13, 47, 64, 67-97,
    156, 160, 181, 184, 204, 208, 213,
    215, 251, 255
Supportive climates, 227
Survey(s), 4, 13, 25, 29, 96, 100, 144,
    147, 148, 149, 189, 202, 203
Structure, 153-158
Sweden, 86, 107
Synapses, 54

Teal, Thomas, 7, 32-33, 35
Teams, 2-3, 6-9, 13, 16-18, 20, 25, 62,
    73, 89, 145, 147-148, 150, 155-156,
    160, 163-193, 197-199, 201, 205,
    229, 242, 248, 252-255
Teamwork, 40, 151
Thailand, 107

UBS, 27
United States, 28, 53, 69 -70, 90,
    110-111, 129, 131, 152, 234, 249
University of California Berkeley, 87
University of Georgia, 91
University of Kalmar, 86
University of London, 84
University of Padova, 90
University of Surrey, 84

University of Virginia, 82, 88
University of Washington, 82

Vanderbilt University, 90
Villages, 23, 87, 128

Wang, Sam, 61
Warterloo University, 84
Waste of knowledge, 144-146
Weber, Max, 16, 134, 140
White, 4, 14, 71, 79, 86, 87, 89-91,
    110, 112-114, 152, 187, 234
White, R.W., 139
Women, 8, 12, 13, 14, 44, 52, 53, 67,
    69, 75-76, 80, 83-84, 85, 87, 88, 90,
    95, 104, 106, 108, 114, 117, 118,
    133, 203, 234

World-class leaders, 5-7, 21-37,
    39-40, 252
World-class products and services, 46,
    156, 176
World-class team, 3, 9, 125, 246, 253
World-class working environment, 20

Xenophobia, 11, 70-72, 105, 110

Yale University, 88
Yugoslavia, 111

Zumwinkel, Klaus, 27

3M, 27

30712452R00155

Made in the USA
Charleston, SC
24 June 2014